FINS
A NOVEL OF RELENTLESS SATIRE

Advanced praise for FINS, A Novel of Relentless Satire

"A hilarious story from a master storyteller with a deep knowledge of marine biology. If you watch 'Jaws' or 'SharkNado' but cheer for the sharks, *FINS* is for you!"

—David Shiffman,
PhD, Author of *Why Sharks Matter*.

"Gruesome and funny in the same scuba breath, *FINS* is rampant with science, corporate intrigue, and outright gore. As in any good parody, the heroine gets her man, and the villains get the hook."

—JoeAnn Hart,
author of *Float*, *Addled*, and *Highwire Act & Other Tales of Survival*

"*FINS* is an ingenious work of biting satire that may trigger a reading frenzy. Great characters and a plot line that never drags. I was hooked after the first chapter."

—Frederic Martini,
PhD, author of *Exploring Tropical Isles and Seas*, *Betrayed*, and *Hounded*.

"A brilliantly presented satire, could not put it down. If you like shark horror stories with a twist, this book is a must."

—Ralph Collier,
author of *Shark Attacks of the Twentieth Century*

"Helfman has woven a wonderfully frenzied tale of killer finless sharks and the misfit crew of people out to protect them. It makes for a fun read and will hopefully spread the word about the terrible practice of shark finning."

—Katherine Maslenikov,
Burke Museum of Natural History and Culture

"Satire uses humor to skewer the bad and deflate the pompous. Good satirists make us think critically while we laugh. I put Gene Helfman in that company. *FINS* is bloody good satire and science fiction."

—Ron Carrol, PhD,
author of *The Spider Talisman*

In *FINS*, Helfman connects science with fiction to produce a humorous, thrilling shark adventure with a great conservation message.

—Gregory Skomal, PhD,
author of *The Shark Handbook* and *Chasing Shadows*.

"Helfman has drawn heavily on his professional scientific knowledge to create this truly unbelievable, but suspenseful comic-like drama. However you feel about sharks now, you might find yourself re-examining your attitude."

—M. A. Marks, PhD,
Founder, Shark Protection and
Preservation Association

"Great characters, great humor, great shark-friendly sharksploitation, great mystery. Keeps you reading straight through to the end. Can't wait for the movie!"

—Richard Brusca, PhD,
award winning author of *In the Land of the
Feathered Serpent* and *The Time Travelers*

"Helfman has succeeded in a difficult enterprise, creating an engaging story using stereotypes for satire, with enough plot interest to make the reader want to know what happens next. A very enjoyable read."

—Harold van Doren,
author of *Lines on the water, An Island
Sense of Home,* and *Survivors*.

"Check out from reality and enjoy Helfman's unique take on the ultimate revenge of the sharks. *FINS* will elicit laughs and maybe some deeper thoughts, but above all, it's just plain fun!"
—JEFFREY CARRIER, PHD,
author of *Sharks of the Shallows*

"Horror and humor, science and satire, a cast of believable good—and really evil—characters, all propelled to a surprise ending by sentient sharks with a single-minded, justifiable goal. *FINS* is the long-needed antidote to *Jaws* and *Sharknado*."
—GEORGE BURGESS,
Curator Emeritus, International Shark Attack File

"Highlights the crucial fishery issue of shark finning [while being] fun reading and thought provoking."
—GREG CAILLIET, PHD,
Director Emeritus, Pacific Shark Research Center,
Moss Landing Marine Laboratories

"An engaging romp through the sharksploitation genre with a world-renowned marine conservationist at the helm. Shark finning: everything is waisted but the fins!"
—LARRY ALLEN, PHD,
former Director, Ocean Studies Institute

Also by Gene Helfman

Fiction

Beyond the Human Realm: A Novel of Love, Loss, and Redemption, Among Whales

Non-fiction

The Diversity of Fishes: Biology, Evolution, and Ecology (with Bruce Collette, Doug Facey, and Brian Bowen)

Fish Conservation: A Guide to Understanding and Restoring Global Aquatic Biodiversity and Fishery Resources

Fishes: The Animal Answer Guide (with Bruce Collette)

Sharks: The Animal Answer Guide (with George Burgess)

FINS

A NOVEL
OF RELENTLESS SATIRE

GENE HELFMAN

LUMINARE PRESS
WWW.LUMINAREPRESS.COM

This is a work of fiction. Any resemblance to actual persons or sharks, living or dead, or actual events is purely coincidental. Names, characters, businesses, places, and incidents are either the products of the author's imagination or used in a fictitious manner. Any inaccuracies throughout the novel, made inadvertently or for the sake of fiction, are my own.

Fins: A Novel of Relentless Satire
Copyright © 2023 by Gene Helfman

All rights reserved. This book or any portion thereof may not be reproduced or used in any manner whatsoever without the express written permission of the publisher, except for the use of brief quotations in a book review.

Printed in the United States of America

Luminare Press
442 Charnelton St.
Eugene, OR 97401
www.luminarepress.com

LCCN: 2023909163
ISBN: 979-8-88679-275-1

To the researchers, policymakers, and environmental advocates who work tirelessly to make the world a better place for sharks and the ecosystems in which they live.

"And Now for Something Completely Different"
MONTY PYTHON'S FLYING CIRCUS

Preface

The lower edge of the blood-red sun touched the ocean's surface. Megan Woodbridge shielded her eyes against the glare. She grew more anxious as she found it harder to pick her slender 7-yr-old daughter's form out from among the larger children. Tatiana tended to gravitate toward older kids because, "I always wanted a big sister."

Tashi floated noticeably as each wavelet passed, the other children still in a depth where they could stand. The shouted taunts of the boys were just audible over the screams of the girls as they exchanged volleys of splashes.

One splash rocketed straight up, higher than the others.

All activity in the water stopped.

"*Did you see that?!*" someone behind Megan shouted.

Author's note: It would have been so easy to just do the above: another predictable shark horror tale, with an inciting incident, conflict (gore), resolution (the mutant shark must die), believable characters (mad scientist, renegade female team member), headed for the Discovery Channel, or worse. But that would have defeated the whole purpose.

Prologue

"Sharks are just more honest and predictable than people."
DR. CHRISTOPHER LOWE,
Calif. State University Long Beach Shark Lab

The great fish moved noiselessly through the dark waters, her mouth slightly open, allowing oxygen-rich water to flow over her massive teeth and gills. Filtered moonlight, broken by occasional clouds, passed down through the water, permitting her to search with all her senses, both the surface above and the upward sloping bottom below. She hadn't eaten in days, twenty-nine to be exact by her count, which was why she had ventured so close to the shore. Her hunger had grown as her two developing young neared their time of release. They needed to be nourished internally, before they turned on one another.

Moving stealthily near the bottom, she heard, then spotted, a creature at the surface. Backlit by the moon, its silhouetted outline came into focus, one of those creatures that moved noisily with two long side fins and two even longer tail fins. Thirty years of experience had convinced her to avoid them. These were enemies she had barely escaped numerous times, when tempted by a variety of dead food they dropped in the water. Embedded inside were sharp, hard, shiny, curved objects that pierced her mouth, often breaking teeth. Their intentions were all too clear. The creature at the surface wasn't worth the risk, despite the ease with which it could be taken. A nice fat seal would do fine and be less problematic. Even a fish would be good, if large enough.

She entered an area that consistently held abundant prey, an anomaly in these depleted waters. Her electrosense told her a stingray was resting on the bottom, probably buried a few inches under the sand, revealed by the pulsing of its breathing. She was swimming leisurely down to grab it, despite its nasty barb (hey, no pain, no gain), when she heard the loud rumble from above.

Looking up, she saw one of the large, pointed shapes that thrashed along the surface, churning it up and leaving a foul-smelling slick. Those tempting, threatening, dead food objects often fell from the same shapes, sometimes on long strings. She turned and, with a powerful sweep of her crescent tail, fled for deeper water.

The kids would just have to work it out between themselves. Time to get the hell out of Dodge.

CHAPTER 1

A run-down fishing boat, white, with numerous rust stains, motored noisily over the glassy water. Moonlight, filtered by diesel exhaust, revealed *Stinky Wrinkle* in fading black letters across its stern. No home port identified.

In the wheelhouse, Agatha Garmin squinted at a video screen that showed the boat's location. A beefy, red-faced woman with short dark hair, Agatha wore full captain's regalia, navy blue with gold tassels and a hat to match. She leaned on a short, odd-shaped, knobby walking stick. Her first mate, a gaunt, tall, dark-bearded man in a yellow slicker and white rubber boots, watched the screen intently.

The chartplotter cast a green glow on their faces. A dashed line on the plotter showed the boat's movement across the water. The boat was headed toward a rectangular area outlined in red. Large letters inside the rectangle read, "**COUSTEAU MEMORIAL MARINE PROTECTED AREA. ABSOLUTELY NO FISHING.**"

"Holy shit, we're fishing there?" the first mate asked, somewhat hesitantly.

"Why not?" replied Agatha. "It's about the only place that still has sharks."

"Hey, you're the captain."

Agatha spit tobacco juice into a small silver spittoon, pulled down a microphone, and bellowed into the intercom, "Get ready to fish, boys. All lights out 'cept red headlamps. Kill the running lights, everything. We're going dark."

Out on the deck, a dozen men, a mix of Asian, Hispanic, and Anglo, scrambled around, preparing the fishing gear. They all sported headlamps, yellow rain gear, and white rubber boots. They tripped over one another in the half-light and swore good-naturedly in their excitement. The men started paying out line off a large drum near the stern, baiting large hooks with malodorous chunks of fish. They tossed the hooks overboard as the line trailed out behind the boat.

The deck crew chief—tall, muscular Rowdy Wagner—reached up to a pole at the end of the line and turned off a blinking light. He flipped another switch as the pole splashed overboard. "Light off, locator activated, and baits on the bottom, Skipper," he spoke into the mike attached to his wide yellow suspenders.

Agatha's voice boomed through an overhead loudspeaker. "Okay. Let's soak those baits for an hour, then haul."

The crew members sat down on nets and buckets, chatted quietly, told jokes, laughed, smoked. Some sharpened long, white-handled knives.

Staring at the chartplotter, Agatha watched a flashing light marked "LAST HOOK," well inside the borders of the protected area. When a digital clock on the screen changed to 2359, an alarm buzzed.

"Okay, boys, time's up. Let's haul 'em in."

Rowdy pulled a hydraulic lever, and the large drum winch started retrieving cable. The first few hooks came aboard, still baited and without fish. Then the first shark appeared.

"Fish on!" Rowdy shouted.

They hauled a large shark aboard and crew members jumped on it, slicing off fins. The shark thrashed about, spurting blood. Severed fins, still alive and trembling, were tossed into a plastic tub, one on top of the other. The shark was slid aside, flailing and bleeding. Every hook came aboard now with an identical shark. The deck was soon covered with bleeding, squirming, finless sharks piled to one side as the tubs filled with quivering fins. The boat reeked of the distinctively metallic odor of blood.

A skinny kid, in his late teens, grabbed a small aluminum baseball bat and approached a shark.

"Hey, Greenie, what the fuck are you doing?" Rowdy shouted.

The kid looked confused, staring at the bat in his hand, then at Rowdy. "I was gonna kill this shark, Rowdy."

"That's not a shark anymore, kid. We call 'em logs after we chop the fins off. The logs go back overboard. Anyway, you can't kill those things. Their brains are too damn small."

"You mean we just dump 'em back while they're still alive?" the kid asked.

"Sure, you gotta problem with that?" Rowdy replied.

"I guess not. They're just dumb-ass sharks, right?"

"Right. So don't lose any sleep over it. They'll be dead soon enough when the crabs and other sharks find them without fins."

The squirming sharks were slid overboard, one after another, the crew sometimes directing a snapping shark at another crewman's feet, seeing who waited the longest to get out of the way. The game was made more challenging as the deck became increasingly slippery from the pools of shark blood.

Rowdy noticed a large shark with a swollen belly lying in the shadows. "Damn. We missed one. You're a big girl, aren't you?" He grabbed a knife and quickly sliced off the shark's side fins. The shark sprang to life, snapping wildly. As Rowdy backed away, the shark lunged over the side, its tail still intact. It joined the other sharks as they thrashed and sank slowly in the bloodstained water, piling up on the bottom. Crabs and hagfish immediately converged on the pile. The tormented sharks twisted and squirmed desperately to avoid being eaten alive.

Back on deck, the crew hosed the fins down, packed them into large plastic boxes, and stacked the boxes on deck. When the catch was stowed, the greenhorn and Rowdy leaned against the stack of boxes, cigarettes in hand.

"Hey, Rowdy. Why don't we cut the logs up and sell shark steaks?"

"Simple economics, kid. It's all about overhead. Steaks take up reefer space and aren't worth much. Fins don't have to be kept cold and are worth a helluva lot more."

The greenhorn, pointing to the fins, asked, "Okay, but who eats this shit?"

"It's all the rage in Hong Kong, 'specially at wedding banquets. It's also 'sposed to be an aphrodisiac, as well as a good luck food. These fins are gonna help some lonesome bachelors at a Chinese wedding get lucky." Rowdy twisted his head and talked into his lapel mike. "We're good down here, Skipper. Catch is stored."

"What's the count?" Agatha asked over the loudspeaker.

"Well, things were happenin' pretty fast, ma'am. We put out thirty hooks and I think only three were empty, so I'd say like twenty-seven sharks, plus or minus."

"Not bad," Agatha said. "At four fins per shark, that's, let's see, one hundred eight. What kind, how big?"

"Kinda weird, ma'am. Hard to tell it bein' dark. Probably sand tigers, all the same kind, all girls, pretty much the same size too, 'cept for one really big momma. And she got away with her dorsal and tail still on."

Agatha hesitated a moment. "Okay. Make it one-oh-six then. No biggee. But it's a little strange. Sandies don't usually live on this coast, and when we do find them, they're usually farther offshore. Maybe they came in shallow to drop pups. But it doesn't matter. We got 'em. I guess there'll be some horny boy sharks in these waters tomorrow."

Agatha opened a thick ledger titled "Catch record, *Stinky Wrinkle*," and wrote down numbers, seemingly at random. She then pulled a tattered journal from under the instrument panel, this one labeled "LOGbook," and recorded a different, more complete set of numbers. Closing the book, she started the engine, turned the boat around and accelerated. As the flashing icon on the chartplotter exited the red-marked reserve area, she flicked running and deck lights back on. The *Wrinkle* disappeared into the night, trailing a dense cloud of foul-smelling black smoke.

CHAPTER 2

Ashley Worth parked her aging, yellow VW Beetle in her assigned spot and turned off the headlights. Ashley was thirty-ish, with long, honey brown hair tied up in a professional ponytail. She walked quickly toward the entrance of an austere, long, low, gray laboratory building. Donning a white lab coat as she hurried along, she looked up at the bold lettering above the entrance, visible in the glow of the parking lot's security lights. The lettering announced "AlphaGen Technologies," followed by the company logo, the Greek letter alpha, two tails of which morphed into a coiled and snaking double helix. The same logo was embroidered across the pocket of Ashley's lab coat.

"Bare us and gird our loins," she whispered.

Inserting her pass key, the door swished open, and Ashley stepped inside. The building smelled of floor wax, clearly the work of Kimo, the night custodian. Walking down a darkened hall, she approached a laboratory door, the only one through which lights shone. This time she punched numbers into a keypad. Locks clicked and she pushed the door open into her home-away-from-home, a lab filled with high-tech equipment.

Flo Takata stood at one of the lab benches, so intent on her work that she didn't hear Ashley enter. Flo also wore an official AlphaGen lab coat, her thin, dark, hair barely reaching her collar. She was concentrating on liquid-filled glassware, adjusting knobs, and didn't even look up.

"Flo, what are you doing here so late, and on a Friday? Oh, I'm sorry, Flo. I didn't mean to scare you."

A startled Flo looked up, and stammered, "Uh, hi, Ashley. I, uh... Just a moment, okay?" She closed a valve. "Mr. Roper told me to make up time. He bawled me out for taking too many bathroom breaks, said I was peeing on company time. He actually knew how many times I went to the ladies' room."

"Ouch!" Ashley responded, clearly disgusted. "That's cringe-worthy. You'd think he had better things to do than spy on us. Sorry to hear that, but if I'm going to work nights, you'd be my first choice for a lab mate."

A clearly embarrassed Flo brushed aside the compliment. "I, uh, guess so. But why are you here at night? I never see you take, uh, potty breaks. Don't you ever take time off?"

"Ironclad bladder, I guess," Ashley said. "But to be honest, I'm mostly trying to get a leg up on the competition. If I can get this Golden Tilapia project done ahead of schedule, Roper will move me from the nosebleed section to the box seats of this operation."

"Well, please wave up at me when you do. I'm just trying to keep my job."

"Firing you would be a dumb move, even for Roper. This lab couldn't function without you."

Flo again brushed off the compliment. "Maybe. Anyway, back to work."

"Yes, back to work," Ashley answered as both women turned to their lab benches, Flo pipetting chemicals, Ashley booting up a computer and instruments.

CHAPTER 3

It was well past midnight Friday, actually early Saturday morning, when the *Stinky Wrinkle* tied up to the commercial docks. The crew unloaded the last of the shark fin-filled plastic tubs, each bearing lettering that read "Flounder Fillets." A foghorn mourned in the distance.

Big Agatha watched over the action from the back of the wheelhouse. "Step lively, lads," she shouted. "Let's get those totes stowed away. I smell rain."

Receiving the tubs was a flatbed truck with "Happy Charlie Seafood" and a cartoonish tuna stenciled on its door. The truck idled, its diesel exhaust competing with the smell of the creosoted dock pilings. A crane lifted the boxes and dropped them in place. The boxes at the top of the stacks vibrated slightly.

"Good work, guys," Rowdy said. "Those flounder fillets will fetch a pretty price. But now it's Miller time. Greenie's buying."

"Hey! What the…!?"

"Fishing's full of traditions, Greenie," Rowdy replied. "It's bad luck to break tradition. Hey, Agatha," he shouted up to the boat. "You gonna join us for a change?"

"Hell no. I spend enough time with you jerks as it is. Someone's got to clean this boat up and get it ready to fish again. And I don't need to watch a bunch of testosterone-poisoned idiots making asses of themselves around the bar tarts."

"She's just jealous," Rowdy said to the greenhorn. "After you, Greenie."

The greenhorn mumbled a weak protest until various crew members slapped him on the back, propelling him along the dock. The assembled crew sped up as the first large raindrops bounced off their heads, the tubs in the departing flatbed truck, and the wheelhouse of the *Wrinkle*. As lightning flashed and thunder rumbled, they all disappeared through swinging doors into a dockside bar where a battered, wind-pushed, creaking sign overhead declared, "THE SPOUTER INN."

Inside the bar, the fishermen, still wearing bloodstained yellow slickers and white boots, stomped across the beer-sodden peanut shells that covered the floor. Various ethnicities moved to separate tables.

The smoke-filled bar resounded with raucous laughter, drowned out by even louder country music from an old jukebox. Waitresses moved between the tables, flirting as much as taking orders, their butts receiving more than a few pinches from the beer-swilling fishermen. As the swilling progressed, bragging about the night's catch intensified to the point that fact and fiction became indistinguishable.

As the carousing intensified, Rowdy stood and ambled off, saying, "'scuse, guys, gotta pump my bilge."

Moments later, one fisherman, then another, turned toward the door, first with puzzled, then with horrified looks. Everything and everyone went quiet, except for the loud music.

The scene quickly turned to carnage. Arms and legs flew, and blood spurted amidst cries of pain as fishermen attempted to flee. The attackers were hidden by cigarette smoke and overturned tables. The waitresses slipped on the concoction of peanut shells, spilled beer, and blood as they rushed to huddle in shock behind the bar.

The attackers fled, still cloaked in smoke, in what appeared as a chain of bodies.

Shortly after, Agatha burst through the door, dripping wet from the downpour, her knobby walking stick in hand. Rowdy emerged from the men's room, zipping up his pants. Both stared at legless and armless torsos strewn about the bar. Agatha bashed the jukebox with her knobby walking stick and the music stopped.

"Jeezus! I heard screaming," she said to Rowdy. "What the hell happened here?"

"Dunno, Skipper. I was in the head, and the music was on in there too. I didn't hear anything." He looked around at the carnage. "Hey! Where are their arms and legs?"

"Damn," she said. "Looks like another crew change on the *Wrinkle*."

CHAPTER 4

Six young Asian couples strolled past neon-lit buildings, shop windows reflecting the bright colors illuminating the strip on a Saturday night. They stopped in front of the pagoda-like storefront of FusionAsia, an upscale Chinese restaurant. The aroma of spices—a mixture of sesame oil and ginger—hung in the air. The couples were ushered into an ornately furnished side room. At low, linen-covered tables already piled with Asian delicacies, they were invited to sit, on the floor. Waiters rolled out carts bearing bowls of soup that were placed with considerable fanfare before the diners.

The manager/head waiter, a short man wearing a dark brown suit, a darker tie, and too much cologne, addressed them in fluent Cantonese. "Tonight, for our distinguished honeymooning guests, to celebrate your lives together and your diving adventure tomorrow, the chef's traditional specialty: shark fin soup."

Several diners exchanged smiles and began to eat with obvious relish. A man said to the woman sitting next to him, "Is this a great country, or what!"

One woman held back. She turned to her companion. "I fought hard when my father tried to serve shark fin soup at our banquet. He wanted to impress business associates he had invited to *our* wedding. I said no, that I was boycotting shark finning. How ironic that we are served it here. I don't want to eat it."

"I agree, honey, but I don't know the customs here in America. Our hosts might be insulted or lose face if we refuse it. Perhaps it's best if we at least pretend?"

"I guess so, still…"

CHAPTER 5

Too early the next morning, the same six Chinese couples, sleepy and burdened with dive gear, climbed onto a dive boat. The boat's engine ran haltingly, black smoke belching from a stack. *"Calypso V—Ultimate Undersea Experience"* was stenciled boldly on its side, the only evidence of recent maintenance.

Luke Fortress, muscular, well-tanned, mid-twenties—a dead ringer for a blond-haired SoCal beach bum—assembled the divers on the stern of the boat for their pre-dive briefing.

"Welcome to the *Calypso*, dudes and dudettes," he announced. "I'm Luke, your divemaster. You're gonna love this trip! We're gonna dive in the Cousteau Sanctuary this morning. I mean the place is crawling with fish and…sharks! It's Shark City and the residents are friendly. So, check your batteries and memory cards. It's gonna be awesome!"

Puzzled, anxious divers stood around listening to Luke. Many didn't understand English, at least not Luke's version. Luke seemed oblivious to their confusion and shouted toward the front of the boat. "Hey, Bubba. Let's get this show on the road."

Bubba Danforth, the current captain of the *Calypso*, stood behind a wooden steering wheel with peeling varnish. Bubba looked to be in the tired part of his forties, sporting wild hair, a scraggly beard, flip-flops, old Bermuda shorts, and a faded flower-print shirt. He pushed a lever forward and the *Calypso*, after a significant period of hesitation, roared to life.

As the boat motored out of the harbor, the divers geared up, donning matching black wetsuits, blue striping for the men, pink for the women. They frequently interrupted their preparations with nervous chatter.

The boat slowed and Luke sprang forward with a boat hook. He snagged a large white buoy marked "Cousteau MPA" and tied up to it. With the divers reassembled on the stern, Luke once again shouted instructions as he strapped a large dive knife to his left leg.

"Awright! Everyone's buddied up, right? Fred here is with me," he said to a solitary diver whose name clearly was anything but Fred. "We'll do a roll call now, and again when you get back. We wanna return with everyone we take out. No repeats from that awful movie, okay? Oh, and please, please, please. Don't pee in your wetsuit. It, like, sends the sharks into a feeding frenzy."

As one couple was about to jump off the boat, the woman turned to the man and gave him an "I-told-you-so" look. He shrugged sheepishly.

"With my bladder infection," she said, "I'll have a helluva time not peeing."

"I thought you took something for that."

"I couldn't get any Ba Zheng San Eight Ingredient Powder to Correct Urinary Disturbances, so I took some tetracycline antibiotic. I'm hoping it's kicked in."

"Well, we'll know for sure," he said, "because I've heard that stuff glows orange in the water."

The divers descended slowly to the bottom. When they touched down, clouds of sediment erupted into the water column, reducing visibility to zero. As the water cleared, they looked around. No fish were visible, only barren sand. They turned in nervous circles while exhaling audibly, and stirred the bottom up again.

Luke scribbled on his dive slate and handed it to his buddy. The scrawl read, "I don't see any damn fish. Do you see any fish?"

Fred shook his head.

Luke's face mask contained a built-in microphone, which allowed him to sort of communicate with the *Calypso*. He shouted, his voice a mixture of words and bubbles. "Hey, Bubba. This sucks. There's nothin' down here. No fish and definitely no sharks. Did we tie up to the right buoy?"

Bubba replied through the speaker in Luke's headset, "Say what? Something fishy on the right by you?"

"No dammit. There's…No…Fish. Did…We…Tie…Up…To…The…Right…Buoy?"

"Of course, we did. Whadda you mean, no fish?"

While this conversation was ongoing, a strong current carried a bright orange cloud of suspended sediment past the divers. One male diver elbowed his female partner, pointed to the orange cloud, and laughed, bubbles exploding from his regulator.

"Like I said, dude," Luke shouted. "There's nothin' down here. Hey, wait!"

"What did you say?" Bubba asked.

One of the divers yanked out his dive knife and started banging on his tank, trying to get everyone's attention. He pointed emphatically at the sediment/dye/odor plume. The other divers turned quickly and looked at the cloud. Dark forms appeared at the edge of visibility, thrashing along the bottom toward them. The excited, panicked movements of the divers stirred up even more sediment. The approaching objects morphed into elongated forms as they entered the cloud, their exact shapes totally obscured.

"Jesus Christ! What the fuck!?" Luke shouted

"Luke! What the hell is going on down there?! Oh my God!" Bubba shouted as he ran to the side of the boat and stared down as a mixture of scuba bubbles and blood boiled to the surface.

Luke appeared out of the bloody, bubbly cloud. He grabbed the lower rung of the boarding ladder, attempting to climb up, despite a scuba tank, weight belt, and a large, dark, obscured shape clamped on his left leg.

As Luke's grip on the ladder began to fail, Bubba grabbed the boat hook and started bludgeoning the thing attached to Luke's leg, hitting it more often than Luke. The thing let go and fell back with a bloody splash. Bubba reached down and barely managed to drag a bleeding Luke aboard.

Both men turned and looked down into the water. No bubbles. Just bloodstained water.

"Damn, I don't think we're covered for this," Bubba mumbled.

"Dude," Luke said. "Call a chopper. I'm, like, dying here."

"Sorry, Luke. We're not supposed to be here. Our permit got pulled 'cause of that thing with the topless honey from Austin. Would've sworn she was at least twenty. I guess lust overcame me. We gotta get away from here first. Hold on, buddy."

Luke fell back on the deck, and the boat took off in a noisy black cloud. Rummaging around for something to act as a tourniquet, Luke spied a hot pink bikini top wedged between two scuba tanks. He looked at it for a moment before tying it around his leg.

Bubba pulled down his radio microphone and screamed, "Mayday, or whatever. We need a medevac at—" he looked at the chartplotter, stammered, corrected himself, "—damn, I can never remember which numbers are our position."

It didn't matter. All the radio produced was static.

"Shit, radio's still on the blink. Meant to fix it last night, but got too wasted. Hey Luke, I'll get you back to the dock soon as I can, buddy. Hold on."

CHAPTER 6

In the AlphaGen laboratory, technicians in white lab coats moved busily about the lab, looking into microscopes, pipetting samples into specimen trays, monitoring outputs from various instruments. Machines whirred, printers printed.

On a shelf above one lab bench sat a row of stainless-steel rat cages labeled "A1," "A2," "B4," and "Blake."

Ashley took the lid off of cage A1, reached in and gently lifted a white rat out by the tail. "Sorry, little guy," Ashley said to the rat. "FDA regulations require we test this stuff on rats. Not that a rat would want to eat it."

She swung the animal hard against the edge of the bench, killing it instantly.

Ashley handed the dead but quivering rat to Flo. "Okay, Flo, I've done the nasty part. Now you can do the dissection."

"Thanks, Ashley. I can't kill them. They're all so sweet."

"No problem, really," Ashley answered. "I just imagine each rat is Roper."

Flo stifled a giggle.

"Anyway," Ashley said. "Your talents are better spent keeping the lab running. We'd be lost without you. You're the only one who remembers the details of all the projects Roper has us juggling."

"I kinda do what I'm supposed to, really," Flo mumbled. "Nothing special."

"You keep doing nothing special, and I'll keep killing rats. For this I got a PhD."

"I guess that's why they pay you the big bucks, right?" Flo said.

"Right. And when I die and go to hell, large, angry rats will grab me by the feet and bash my head against a rock for all eternity."

Ashley absentmindedly reached into the cage labeled "Blake" and picked up a distinctive, black-and-white rat by the tail. She was about to bash it but stopped.

"Blake, honey," she said. "What are you doing on death row? Hey guys! Who put Blake on death row!?"

Various technicians in white lab coats looked around, but mostly at their feet.

"Blake, sweetie, you almost bought the farm."

Ashley placed the rat on her shoulder. The rat quickly scampered down the front of her lab coat.

"Blake, you naughty, naughty boy."

Clive Moulton, AlphaGen's painfully-thin, geeky, African American, IT specialist was working at a nearby terminal, helping someone with a computer issue, but covertly paying attention to Ashley and the rat cage snafu. He mumbled to himself, "Oh, Lord, please, please, kill me right now and bring me back as a white rat. Better yet, make that a black-and-white rat."

"Good morning, AlphaGentlemen and Women," came the announcement over the facility's intercom. All activity stopped as the assembled staff turned to a speaker above a TV set in the lab. The voice of D. W. Roper, President and CEO of AlphaGen, was easy to recognize.

"Oh boy," Ashley said. "AlphaGentlemen's a new one. I wonder what Captain Cliché's platitude-laced Monday morning pep talk will be this time?"

One of the technicians hurriedly passed out pieces of paper and pencils to everyone.

Roper cleared his throat. "Here on the AlphaGen Campus, where we're all part of the AlphaGen ecosystem, we're a team, a big family,"

"Albeit dysfunctional," someone muttered.

"…working diligently to bring several projects to completion. And for me, as it is for all of us, top to bottom, I take special pride in our Golden Tilapia effort. Let me unpack the importance to you, drill down to its essence. Golden Tilapia represents a paradigm shift in food science. I've done the necessary due diligence here, and I know we have a roadmap to an off-ramp to its successful completion."

"Ropero!" someone shouted.

"Damn, I was one short," someone else remarked.

"So, let's bring this baby home now," Roper continued. "Thank you. As you were."

The assembled AlphaGen family turned back to their various waystations on the highway to fame and fortune.

"Who got the Ropero?" Ashley asked.

A female tech in a white lab coat, back of the room, said, "Five across: campus, family, AlphaGen logo free space in the center, unpack, paradigm shift."

"Sounds good," Ashley said. "Parking space number one, closest to the exit, is yours for the week. Someone make sure AlphaGentlemen gets added to the cards."

After a few seconds of applause, everyone resumed their work.

But activity ground to another halt when a female voice announced over the facility's intercom, "Ashley Worth, Ashley, you have a phone call."

"Dammit," Ashley said out loud. "I don't need another

interruption." She gently pulled the rat from inside her lab coat and placed it back in its cage. "Somebody please put Blake back in the rat room. And please tie a red ribbon around his cage so he doesn't have another near-death experience."

Ashley glanced nervously at instruments beeping at her station. She picked up a large handbag and started to leave the lab when Roper's forceful voice broke in over the intercom.

"Miss Worth, make this quick! You're on the clock."

Various technicians glanced at each other sympathetically.

Ashley hurried down a corridor to the lobby reception area. She stopped in front of Talulah Jones, the fashionably dressed, 30-ish African American receptionist. Talulah handed Ashley a phone.

"Hello? This is Ashley Worth. Luke? Why are you calling me at work? Why are you calling me at all? I told you. We're through, finished, it's over."

Ashley listened for about fifteen seconds, her expression changing from anger to alarm.

"Oh, my God! You're kidding. A shark? Your leg? Where are you? I'll leave right now!"

Roper's voice cut in through a speaker mounted next to a video camera over Talulah's desk. "Miss Worth! Where are you going? We have a contract and a deadline. You cannot leave."

Looking up at the surveillance camera, Ashley whispered to Talulah, "That's kind of creepy. Those things are everywhere."

"And Roper has a feed to all of them," Talulah remarked. "I spend the entire day under his loving, watchful gaze."

"That bastard," Ashley said. "Given what Flo told me last night, I wouldn't be surprised if he's watching the bathrooms."

"The word going around," Talulah answered, "is you're his favorite."

Ashley paused a moment. "Next time, I'll remember to moon him."

"That would make his day."

Ashley scribbled on a Post-it Note, handed it to Talulah. "Medical emergency. Here's my cell number. You can tell Roper I'll make up the time tonight."

"Not Luke again?" Talulah asked.

"Yeah, I'd be better off adopting a rescue dog. Why do I have such phenomenally bad taste in men?"

"Ashley, hon. You're a member of a very big club."

CHAPTER 7

Ashley pulled into the parking lot of the regional hospital and walked through the emergency entrance doors. At the nurse's station, she was directed to Luke's room. Not knowing what to expect but fearing the worst, she entered quietly to find Luke with his leg in traction and a drip attached to his arm.

"Hi, beautiful. Thanks for coming," Luke said in a drowsy voice.

"Against my better judgment," she replied. "Were you chumming for sharks again, dummy?"

"No, nothing like that," Luke answered. "We stopped doing that stuff after we lost that lawyer from LA. We were diving in the reserve, legally of course, and it was, you know, like weird right from the start."

"Weird? Like how weird?"

"Well, first there was nothing there. I mean, like, usually the place is lousy with fish. But there was nothing and then—" he shuddered, "—these sharks showed up from down current and, like, they were totally weird. They were all alike, and didn't have fins, and, like, squirmed across the bottom, you know, like a team, and they circled us like a team, and—"

"Whoa. Hold on a minute, Luke. Sharks don't squirm, they swim. I thought you stopped smoking before a dive."

"Swear to God, Ashley. I wasn't high. All at once, the sharks attacked us. Like on a signal."

"Us?"

"Oh yeah, almost forgot. We had a tour group of like a dozen or so foreign divers."

"What kind of foreign?"

"Asian, I think. They were Chinese, or Korean, or something. I never really looked at their names. Not that I would have known."

"Great. And where are they now?"

"Not really sure. Things happened kinda fast."

"Luke! You abandoned your dive customers? I don't believe it. No, I do believe it. That's totally irresponsible and…racist."

"Hey, at that point it was every Luke for himself. Look at me. It's not like I wasn't part of the meal plan. One of those creeps grabbed my leg 'til Bubba smashed it with something." Then Luke started mumbling, "Hey, babe, I'm gettin' kinda sleepy here. Thanks for coming."

"Right. Get better." Under her breath she added, "Squirming sharks. Right."

CHAPTER 8

A nondescript, two-story, dirty brick warehouse sat between equally nondescript buildings in a run-down section of the docks. The warehouse office, accessible from the street by a metal staircase, overlooked a floor area. Below, workers labored among blood-covered tables, trimming shark fins and packing them in foam boxes. Every now and then, a fin quivered.

In the office, the fiftyish, greasy-haired owner and a bespectacled accountant, wearing a white shirt and green transparent visor, studied a computer screen.

The owner flipped a switch on a display panel and shouted, "What's happening down there? Aren't you guys done yet?"

After a delay, one of the workers answered via the intercom, "Yeah, boss. We're taping up the last boxes now. Should be able to ship tomorrow."

"This damn spreadsheet is too fucking complicated," the owner said to the accountant. "Run some numbers by me that I give a fuck about."

"Okay. The last quote we got on trimmed fins was $93.76 a pound."

"Hot damn! That I understand. What about meat without fins?"

The accountant scrolled down the page on the screen. "About a buck a pound."

"I thought so. Same fuel and bait costs, and fins don't need to be refrigerated. That slashes my overhead. It's a win-win in my books, proves I'm a financial wizard."

"Let's just hope Mr. R is as happy," the accountant offered.

"Hey. He gets the fins, we get the cash, no one loses. Except maybe the sharks. But fuck 'em, the brainless brutes."

As if on cue, the door from the stairwell burst open. Both men swiveled around and froze in horror. In an attempt to get up from his rolling chair, the owner became tangled in a phone cord, ripping it from the control panel, which shorted the master circuit and plunged the building into darkness. He fell over the accountant, both tumbling to the floor behind the desk. They threw their hands up to cover their faces.

Screams filled the office, legs and arms flew.

The workers below heard the commotion upstairs and looked up in shock at the office but could make out nothing in the dim light. Dark, elongated shapes dropped from the catwalk, landing on the tables, knocking the workers to the floor.

Amid piercing screams, disembodied arms and legs lay scattered around the tables. In the confusion, a fire broke out when a lit cigarette landed in a pile of oily rags.

As the conflagration grew, the dark shapes quickly escaped through a side door, their identity obscured by the smoke. The partially functional automated sprinkler system slowly sprang to life, dowsing the flames.

CHAPTER 9

Slipping on her lab coat, Ashley entered AlphaGen again and stopped at Talulah's desk.

"How's the Luke?" Talulah asked. "Are you two back together?"

"Please, Talulah, don't start any rumors. I'm more fed up with him than ever."

"Too bad," Talulah said. "If you're willing to overlook some fatal flaws, he's quite a hunk."

"More like an attractive nuisance," Ashley remarked.

"So, what's the medical emergency?" Talulah asked. "Will he live?"

"Only if he stays away from me. Basically, he's okay, I guess. Pretty sedated."

"Nothing new."

"Granted, but he told me the strangest story."

"Again, nothing new. Please give me the gory details later. Meanwhile, Mr. Groper requests your presence."

"Expected."

Ashley approached a textured glass-and-wood office door, the name "D. W. Roper, President and CEO" stenciled on the glass. She knocked softly.

"Come in."

Ashley stood inside the door, clearly unwilling to go farther. "Mr. Roper, you wanted me?"

Roper sat ramrod straight behind a large, polished-wood desk, empty except for a phone, computer screen, and keyboard. He was appropriately attired for a slimeball fifty-year-old CEO: tanned, tailored suit and tie, dark hair in a one-hundred-dollar haircut with gray streaks on the sides. The room was richly paneled in unsustainably harvested tropical hardwood. Modern art hung on the walls.

Roper smiled lasciviously at Ashley. "So nicely phrased, Ashley. Please, come sit down."

"Thank you, sir, but I really need to get back to my work. I'm sorry I ran off. It was a medical emergency."

Roper's tone changed, becoming threatening. "Exactly, Ashley. You know, Ashley, the Golden Tilapia project is vitally important to AlphaGen. I'm hoping we're on the same bandwidth here, that you're not pivoting to other projects. I'd look unfavorably, Ashley, at further interruptions to your work. You get my drift?"

"It's clear, sir. We are so close to a solution. And no one wants to see that work finished more than I do. Really."

Ashley turned and left, and Roper smiled at her backside. His fantasy about requiring the women wear tighter lab coats was interrupted when his phone buzzed. He pushed a button.

"What?"

"Mr. Roper," Talulah said through the speaker on Roper's desk. "Mr. Chang is on the line."

"Damn! Okay, Lulu, put him on."

Talulah responded emphatically, "It's Talulah, Mr. Roper, and always has been."

"Whatever." Roper pushed a flashing button on his desk set and picked up the receiver. "Hello, Mr. Chang, good to hear from you, sir."

An angry, mumbling voice could be heard through the phone.

"Yes, sir, Mr. Chang. I'm totally aware of that and of the consequences. It's our top priority, sir. I've got our best people working on it 24/7, sir."

More angry mumbling through phone.

"We're on that, too, sir. The, er, flounder shipment should be going out in a day or so, as soon as the truck gets here."

More mumbling on the phone.

"Thanks for calling, sir. I'll get right back to work on that, right now."

Roper jerked the phone away, a loud bang from the other end obviously hurting his ear. He pushed a button on the handset and the light blinked off. Roper waited a good five seconds, making sure the line was dead.

"And goodbye to you too, a-hole."

Reaching into the desk drawer, Roper took out a jar of antacid, gulped a handful, and chased it with a pull from a Chivas bottle.

CHAPTER 10

Late that evening, a tired Ashley stood at her lab bench, mechanically processing samples. The laboratory was otherwise empty. Her computer screen indicated "mitochondrial DNA sequence, Read 472," followed by lines of code and a complex graph. A nearby TV was tuned to a news channel, the sound audible but indistinct.

All the squiggly lines on her analytical machine went flat. In a panic, Ashley frantically mashed her keyboard. The machine responded with a pulsing, alarm-like buzz.

"Dammit, dammit, dammit!"

She dashed to a phone on the wall below the TV, anxiously scanned a list of numbers and names, and punched buttons.

A phone rang in the nearby IT room, where computers, server units, and a spaghetti-like maze of multicolored cable competed for space with empty pizza boxes and energy drink cans. The only person in the room was IT specialist Clive Moulton. Moulton, wearing a virtual reality headset and headphones, was playing a video game, "Shark Attack 3D." The phone rang repeatedly for a full minute before he reacted.

Reluctantly, Clive answered the phone, still wearing the headset. His tone suggested less than a nanogram of enthusiasm. "This is tech, hold on a minute."

Clearly annoyed at the interruption, Clive finished a game sequence and finally took off the VR headset.

"Okay. Where were we?" he said.

"Hello, tech support? Hi, uh, this is Ashley Worth in the sequencing lab."

Clive came to attention.

"My automatic sequencing machine blew up in the middle of a Golden Tilapia run. I'm getting garbage sequences. I don't know if it's the capillaries, the fluoroscope, the software, or what. I desperately need help. Badly."

"Uh, right, of course, sure. Happy to, um, ah, help."

"Oh, thank you!" Ashley gushed into the phone.

Clive jumped up, slicked his hair, tucked in his shirt, and knocked over a can of energy drink, splashing it onto his pants. Looking down, cursing, he left the room.

Clive entered Ashley's lab, clearly nervous and totally awestruck.

"Um, uhh. Hi A-Ash-Ashley. What's the problem?"

"Oh, hi, Clive. I'm really sorry to be bothering you so late."

"Um, uhh. Not a problem, not a problem. Glad to here be, uh, be here. I mean, I'm happy it's me here and you here and…uh. Um…" He muttered to himself, "Damn!"

"Clive," Ashley began in a sweet voice. "I'm running the DNA sequencing analysis prior to a critical gene splice for the tilapia contract, and Roper's on my case to get it done, and now my automatic sequencing machine is spewing out nonsense."

Clive, a little more comfortable now, and sensing an opportunity to become familiar with Ashley, said, "Yeah, He-who-shall-not-be-named sent Flo home in tears this afternoon for mislabeling one of the add-read-unblock cycle samples for the tilapia thing."

"Flo? He jumped on Flo? She's a godsend, the best tech in the lab. She's just shy."

"We all know that," Clive said. "She tried to explain to Roper that someone else must have entered the wrong info on a sample spreadsheet, but he wouldn't listen. He tore her a new one right in front of the whole lab."

"That's totally unfair," Ashley said. "Roper picks on Flo because he knows she won't fight back. He's a class-A bullying cowardly asshole. He should stay out of the lab and let us do our work."

"He's definitely worked up about that tilapia project," Clive concurred. "That's why I'm on the night shift, just in case something like this happens. Let me look."

"Oh, thank you, Clive."

Clive twisted knobs, peered around at the cables snaking out of the instrument, said, "Hmm, oh, aha," then adjusted something. Moving to Ashley's keyboard, his fingers flew across the keys. He stepped back. "Okay. Let's give it a go, ho-ho."

Ashley moved back to her position in front of the lab bench, gently brushing against Clive, who jumped as if jolted by electricity. She pushed one button. Lights flashed and things returned to normal.

"Thank God. You're a genius, Clive."

"We who toil in the depths of the IT dungeon live only to serve. Ha-ha. So anyway, what's all the fuss over this Golden Tilapia project?"

"It's pretty much cookbook gene splicing," Ashley said. "We're inserting a gene from bacteria that live in Norwegian eels and putting it into a food supplement for tilapia fish to see if the genes can jump from the Norwegian eels to tilapia. Pretty routine genmod technology, really."

"Seems like kind of basic science for a predatory capitalist like Roper," Clive offered. "It has to make money somehow, don't you think, or Mr. Greed-Is-Good wouldn't be so tied into knots over it."

"Well, if it works, the tilapia will grow faster on the same amount of food and reach marketable size sooner, thus increasing protein availability. At least according to Roper. And maybe people would equate our genetically modified tilapia with the health benefits of eating cold-water fish, like salmon. Plus, I think that's where the 'golden' part comes in. It's some kind of marketing ploy. Any fish with golden in its name sells better. So, we're also putting a color additive in the feed to give the flesh a yellow tinge. It's like they do with pink dye in farmed salmon."

"I guess 'gray tilapia' isn't going to exactly fly off the shelves, eh?" Clive said.

"Marketing's not my concern," Ashley replied. "I'm in charge of modifying stuff in petri dishes, so it won't break down during digestion. It has to do with bacteria and jumping genes, my area of expertise. What they do with it later isn't in my job description, way above my pay grade."

"Right. Once the rockets go up, who cares where they come down."

Clive was enjoying the interaction. He climbed up on a lab stool and rotated to face Ashley. "So, did you always want to be a genetic technology wizard?"

"Oh no, not at all. After I got over horses and dolphins and unicorns, I wanted to be a reporter."

"And?"

"I co-majored in English and journalism in college, and, *voila*, landed a journalism job."

"Wow! Like with the *Times* or the *Post*?"

"Not even close. I became a reporter for one of the supermarket checkout stand tabloids."

"Hmm. Not quite prime time, I guess. Which one?"

"It doesn't matter, really," Ashley answered. "They're all basically interchangeable."

"Cool," Clive said. "I pass up the self-checkout aisle so I can read the bombshell headlines: Kurt Cobain was depressed. Woody Allen was kinky. Michael Jackson was weird. Elvis had an eating disorder. Very edifying. So, you stalked celebrities?"

"Didn't have to. They're needy, insecure, tortured souls who can never get enough attention. They stalked us. I wrote the cycle stories: seen dating, engagement, lavish wedding, baby bump, weight gain, diet pill addiction, affair with the nanny, ugly divorce. Same celebs, same stories, lather, rinse, repeat."

"Apparently you didn't stick with it?"

"Right. After a while, I got bored. I wanted something more meaningful. I read about medical breakthroughs using genetic engineering. I went back to school, aced the science and math classes I'd avoided my first round of college, and went to grad school in genetics. Got my doctorate and Roper immediately hired me at AlphaGen."

Ashley's attention was drawn to jostling and shouting on the TV, where picketers were carrying hastily made placards outside a restaurant. The placards said, "Finning is murder," "Stop Finning," "Sharks belong in the sea, not the soup." Some placards showed photos of stacks of shark fins and finless sharks lying on the ocean bottom.

The camera swung to a neatly dressed newscaster wearing a yellow blazer with "KNSX TV NEWS" across his chest. He spoke into a handheld microphone.

"This is Stan Daily, KNSX News, reporting live outside an upscale restaurant downtown, where the Friends of Sharks have brought their anti-finning campaign." He turned to interview a short-haired female protestor. "What is it you folks hope to accomplish here?"

The protestor was wearing a t-shirt with "PESTO" printed in large block letters, under which was written, "Fish are our friends, not our food."

Daily pointed the mike at her. She cleared her throat and launched into a well-rehearsed polemic.

"FusionAsia is the only restaurant downtown that still serves shark fin soup. Fishermen catch sharks, cut off their fins, and throw them back in the water, alive...like seventy million a year. All to make soup for rich customers in China and Singapore, and FusionAsia Restaurant, even though eating shark fins is a health hazard because they contain a lot of mercury. It's cruel and unusual and barbaric...and... and just plain stupid. We in People for the Ethical, Sensitive Treatment of Organisms plan to picket FusionAsia until they stop serving shark fin soup."

Daily looked at her t-shirt. "Are sharks fish?"

"Yes, dummy. What? Did you flunk biology?"

"Never had to take it. Regardless, I think you've got a pretty hard sell here. Public sympathy doesn't often lie with sharks."

"That's because the public is made up of other flesh-eating dummies that watch sensationalized TV news channels like yours."

"Hmmm. Well, that's it from The Strip. This is Stan Daily, KNSX News, reporting live downtown. Back to you, Rupert."

Ashley turned to Clive and asked, "What was that all about?"

"It's been all over the news," he answered. "You haven't seen it before?"

"No. I've been slaving over a hot chromatograph 24/7 for two weeks. If we bring this Golden Tilapia project in on time and budget, I'll move up from technician to senior analyst, with a big pay raise."

"Well," Clive said. "It's all about a campaign to stop shark finning. Apparently, shark fin soup is a real delicacy in Hong Kong and places like that. A gelatinous bowl of shark fin soup can cost, like, a hundred bucks. It's all part of some business or social tradition, showing off you can afford it."

"Yuk," Ashley said. "Sharks give me the creeps. I can't imagine eating them. I won't go near the water because of them."

She turned back to her instruments and Clive muttered to himself, "The beach is the poorer for that."

Ashley stopped and reflected for a moment, then said, "Anyway, nobody is finning sharks around here, are they?"

"Naw. It's against the law here. They do it in China and Taiwan and those places."

"Good, it does sound kind of gruesome."

"Yeah, if you care about sharks," Clive said.

"Not really. Anyway, I've got to get back to my hot chromatograph. Thanks again so much, Clive."

"Anytime. Really."

CHAPTER 11

The charter sportfishing boat *Happy Hooker* motored offshore, fishing lines streaming out behind. The Sunday morning fishing party onboard consisted of several middle-aged business types in aloha shirts, loud Bermuda shorts, and black socks. They were accompanied by young, bikini-clad women—some, perhaps, of negotiable virtue—several lounging up front, while others perched and posed near the stern. Alcohol was in abundance.

Three husky, tanned crew members stood at the ready, tending the fishing lines. One crew member, positioned near the stern, studied the fishing lines while talking to a paunchy, sun-burnt client.

"Is this a good place to catch something?" the client asked.

"Yes sir. Cap'n Lewmar is the best. Right now, we're fishing the boundary of the Cousteau Protected Area. It's a good spot, because fish spill over from the preserve."

No sooner had he spoken when one of the rods almost leapt out of its holder. Line ran out so fast the reel screamed. Several crew members jumped up, reeled in the other lines, shouted orders. They strapped the paunchy fisherman into the fighting chair and handed him the rod.

"Start reeling and pumping and keep the rod tip up at all times," he was told.

The instantly out-of-breath client started cranking on the reel handle and broke into a sweat. "Whoa Nelly! It's a big one. What have I got?"

"Could be a marlin, or a swordfish, or—*keep the damn rod tip up!*—a sailfish, or a mahi-mahi, or a wahoo, or—"

The line suddenly went slack.

"Damn! He got off," the client said, between gasps.

"No, keep reeling," he was instructed. "Sometimes they run straight at the boat. Reel like crazy or we could lose him."

A large shark, finless except for its tail, with the fishing lure in its mouth, leapt over the stern and onto the boat. It immediately chomped down on the leg of the client, who couldn't escape because he was strapped into the fighting chair. More finless sharks followed over the stern in a daisy chain of sharks, each holding onto the tail stump of the shark ahead of it. Crew members, clients, and accompanying women got tangled in the fishing lines and also couldn't escape.

Arms and legs were severed.

One shark bit through the fishing line, releasing the shark that had been hooked.

Crew members grabbed anything they could find and started clubbing the sharks, which departed hastily, some with body parts in their mouths.

Captain Lewmar, up in the wheelhouse, had been watching the mayhem. "Jesus Christ! Did I see what I just saw?" He grabbed a microphone and started shouting, "Mayday! Mayday! Shark attack! This is the *Happy Hooker*. We've had an accident, several persons severely injured. We need immediate medical assistance."

Without delay, a voice answered his call. "*Happy Hooker*, this is the Coast Guard. What is your position?"

"We are about a mile off the north end of the Cousteau Preserve, ten persons on board, at least four are injured."

"We are scrambling a rescue chopper. Please stay where you are and remain calm. The chopper should be there in… fifteen minutes."

"Remain calm my ass," Lewmar replied. "I've got a shit show on my hands! You should see the clusterfuck on my stern."

"This is an open channel, Captain. Please watch your language."

"Get that damned chopper here pronto…and go to hell. My taxes pay your goddam salary."

The Coast Guard chopper arrived and hovered over the boat. Its well-trained crew lifted one, then another, person in the rescue basket. Captain Lewmar insisted on riding along and was the last to be lifted. The chopper tilted and accelerated toward shore. It descended onto the landing pad of the regional hospital. Orderlies with gurneys were lined up and waiting. They unloaded the victims and rushed inside.

Captain Lewmar left the chopper, where he was met by the newscaster who had reported on the anti-finning protest.

"This is Stan Daily live from Mercy Hospital where four patients have just been admitted following a shark attack on the sportfishing boat *Happy Hooker*. The *Hooker*'s captain, Ralph Lewmar, is with me. Can you tell us what happened Captain Lewmar?"

"Damndest thing I've ever seen," Lewmar said, his voice shaking. "We got a strike on the number three line and reeled in a shark. Actually, we didn't reel it in, we hooked it and it jumped on board. Then it attacked the guy in the chair. And then other sharks followed, a line of them, one after another, and started biting folks. They were all females, didn't have that shark penis thing. And they were all finless. Except for one that looked like it had legs. I dunno. But mostly they wiggled around and bit people. It was a bloodbath. The crew fought back, and then the sharks all jumped off the boat as fast as they boarded her. Damndest thing I've ever seen."

"Thank you, Captain. The hospital isn't releasing names until next of kin can be notified. We will stand by with developments. Stan Daily, KNSX News, reporting live from Mercy Hospital. Back to you, Penny."

Ashley Worth scurried around her clearly downscale, cluttered, post-grad school apartment, gulping coffee as she readied to go to work. Her TV was tuned to a Sunday morning news show when the broadcast was interrupted by the bulletin from Mercy Hospital. She stopped and listened, puzzled, indecisive. Finally, picking up her phone, she said to herself, "What the hell. Roper doesn't pay me overtime. His damn tilapia can wait."

She punched numbers into her phone.

Clive Moulton's apartment, in contrast, was modern and spartan, dominated by a black leather sofa and an expansive big-screen TV. On either side of the TV were huge stereo speakers and two life-size cardboard cut-outs, one of a teenage Harry Potter and the other of Steve Jobs. Clive sat on the sofa, game console in hand, engaged in a loud, multi-player video game. A pop-up message appeared on the screen: "INCOMING CALL FROM A. WORTH."

Surprised, Clive paused the game and hit a button on the console.

"Uh, hello?"

"Hello, Clive? Hi, it's Ashley," her voice boomed through the stereo speakers.

"Hey, hold on a moment," he said. He turned the volume down on the console. "Ashley?"

"Yes. Ashley Worth, from work."

"Really?"

"Yes, that Ashley. You said you could help me anytime. So, I need your help."

"Really? Wow! I mean sure, er, just name it."

"Why thank you, Clive, but it's complicated and you may not be quite so willing after I explain things. I know it's Sunday, but could you possibly meet me at the lab?"

"At the lab? Of course, at the lab."

"Great. I'll be there in, say, twenty minutes. Thank you, Clive, so much."

Ashley parked her VW next to Clive, who was already waiting in a faded, two-tone pink Ford Bronco with a white top. He got out hurriedly, stumbling slightly, explaining quickly as he recovered, "Um. Ah. This, this isn't my car. My uh… Tesla's in the shop, getting some warranty work done. Didn't think I'd be going out this weekend. This is my sistah's, I mean sister's."

"Clive, it's really, really nice of you to meet me here on a Sunday. And please, thank your sister for loaning you her car. I know it's an inconvenience for both of you."

"No problem, no problem at all. What's the big mystery? It seemed like all the lab systems were go on Friday. I checked the readouts I have from your lab before I left Friday night."

Ashley looked around at an otherwise-empty parking lot. "Thank you for watching out for our work, Clive. I really appreciate it. But this thing today isn't really a work-related problem. At least I don't think it is. But the lab seemed like a good place to meet. Let's go inside and I'll tell you all about it."

In her lab, Ashley started to explain, "Clive, you know that news report we watched the other night, about the protestors?"

"Oh yeah. You mean the eco-anxious fish huggers at that restaurant?"

"Yes, them. You didn't happen to watch the news this morning?"

Clive's answer was a little sheepish, as if he'd been caught doing something juvenile. "Um, no, I was, um, playing a video game online when you called."

Ashley walked over to the TV on the wall. "Let's see if there's an update on today's events."

The TV came on and, sure enough, it was Stan Daily.

"… here at Mercy Hospital, where, about an hour ago, four shark attack victims with multiple injuries were brought by helicopter. Unfortunately, one has died and the other three are in critical condition. Otherwise, we don't have much information. But here's a re-broadcast of our earlier interview with the captain of the fishing boat involved in the incident."

The unmistakable image of Captain Lewmar loomed on the screen.

"And then other sharks followed and started biting folks. They were all females, didn't have that shark penis thing. And they were all finless. Except for one that looked like it had legs. I dunno. But mostly they wiggled around and bit people. It was a bloodbath. The crew fought back and then the sharks all jumped off the boat as fast as they boarded her. Damndest thing I've ever seen."

"Oh-kay," Clive said slowly. "Where's this leading?"

"Well, a…er…um friend of mine was also attacked by finless sharks, like a week ago. Bitten on the leg like the folks on that fishing boat. He also said the attack seemed organized. While my, um, friend is frequently unreliable, the two stories are so alike that I tend to believe him. I think there's a connection. Maybe it's my journalism training kicking in. Or maybe it's nothing. Maybe I should just forget about it."

"No, no. I think you're right," Clive answered, clearly not wanting the opportunity to be with Ashley to end prematurely. "It does sound like a weird coincidence. But what do you think we should do about it?"

"I guess we could go down to the docks and ask some questions, try to separate fact from fiction. There could be more to this than the news reports are revealing, or even know."

"Awesome! I mean absolutely, that's a good place to start. I was getting trounced online by a guy in Kiev anyway. Time to overcome an addictive distraction, cut my losses, declare victory, and leave. Plus, this sounds like more fun, and I've always wanted to be a sleuth."

CHAPTER 12

Riding in Clive's sister's pink and white Bronco "because it's less obvious, or at least less threatening," Ashley and Clive drove to the docks. Ashley had a little difficulty squeezing into the passenger's seat, which was pushed far forward to make room for a saddle that took up much of the back. In fact, the entire rear storage space was full of equestrian gear, the car smelling of horse manure-tinged leather.

"My sister's a bit of a horse nut," Clive explained. "Always has been. It's kind of her identity. She's president of the Black Equestrian Association. That's why she got a very used Bronco. She wanted a Mustang, but economics and storage room were an issue."

It was a straight shot to the docks except for a stop sign at an intersection that required crossing a busy highway. Old Broncos weren't known for spaciousness, and with the right-hand seat pushed forward, Ashley blocked most of Clive's view of oncoming traffic from the right.

"Is it clear?" he asked, trying to peer around her.

"Truck," Ashley replied.

Clive accelerated into the intersection.

"*STOP!*"

Clive slammed on the brakes as a speeding cement mixer swerved around them, its horn blaring, leaving the Bronco and its occupants shaking.

Clive crossed the intersection slowly, then pulled over. Both occupants tried to calm their nerves.

Finally, Ashley said, "I told you a truck was coming! You could have got us killed!"

Clive, still feeling that he might be on tentative ground, stifled any anger. "I thought you told me to truck, so I did."

"What?" Ashley asked incredulously.

"Ashley, where I grew up, in the 'hood, in South Central LA, truck is a verb."

"And where I grew up in Indiana, and in most of the fly-over states, truck is a noun."

They sat in silence for about ten seconds, then both broke out laughing.

"Culture clash," Clive finally said. "I guess we'll just have to be on guard, stick to simple yes-no questions."

"Could be a challenge," Ashley said. "But it's good to know I'm finally tall enough for Mr. Toad's Wild Ride."

Clive breathed another sigh of relief and pulled out onto the road.

The remainder of the drive was blessedly uneventful. They arrived at the docks, which were eerily devoid of people. After a few wrong turns and dead-end alleys, they found a warehouse they suspected might be a promising place to start, given the trail of blood leading to an open door.

Ashley entered first, hesitantly. Clive followed, even more hesitantly.

The interior was dark, a smell of quenched fire unmistakable. Standing barely inside, Clive's resolve collapsed, and he turned to leave, but Ashley grabbed his arm. Using her cellphone flashlight, she located a light switch.

The scene that greeted them was one of total chaos, a disaster. Limbless bodies lay scattered around tables on which Styrofoam boxes sat, several askew, their lids taped shut.

"Oh my god! What happened here?" Ashley whispered.

"This was one party I'm glad I didn't get invited to," Clive said.

"They're, like, dismembered," Ashley said. "Their arms and legs are gone! Are they all…dead?"

"Looks like it," Clive answered. "Could have been a drug deal gone bad. I'll bet there's drugs in those boxes."

He took a tool from his ever-present utility belt, slit the tape on one box, lifted the lid. "Naw, no drugs, just shark fins. Boy, do they stink!"

"Shark fins? You're kidding." She looked inside the box. "Nope, you're right."

One torso moved and moaned.

"Hey, this guy's alive," Clive exclaimed. "Hey, man, what happened?"

"The sh…sh…sharks. They attacked us. It was terrible. They all came in at once, squirming across the floor. Their eyes were glowing. They bit off arms and legs. My legs! Where are they? I…I…"

He fell back, eyes staring into space.

"I guess they are *all* dead," Clive said.

"This is terrible," Ashley said. "It's worse than terrible, like out of some horror movie, except we're in it, for real. We should call the police, or an ambulance, or someone."

"I think we should get the hell out of here before the sharks come back."

"I guess so," Ashley said. "We can call the police later. But I want to take some of these fins. This is just too weird."

"What? Are you going to make soup?"

"No, I want to do what I always do. Run some analyses.

Maybe it will help explain this…weirdness."

She picked up a small box and they left the building.

"Oh boy. Nancy Drew, forensic pathologist," Clive mumbled.

They exited the building slowly, Clive looking left and right.

"Is shark a verb too?" Ashley quipped.

Ashley put the box in the back of the Bronco. As she closed the liftgate, the box jiggled slightly, unnoticed.

A few minutes down the road, Ashley said, "Clive, pull over here and I'll call."

"I think," Clive responded, "it's probably safe to drive and call if I'm driving and you're calling. Really."

"It's not that, silly. I just don't want to go too far from the warehouse. I want to go back there and watch what the police do."

With the car pulled off the road, Ashley dialed 9-1-1. "Yes, I want to report a…an incident… No, I'm okay… Yes, this is an emergency, or at least it was… I am calm… No, I don't need help. We…I…My name isn't important. Listen, send police to the old warehouse at the commercial docks. I think there's been a murder."

Ashley hung up and they sat in the car, waiting.

Clive finally broke the silence. "Pardon me for asking, Ashley, but is what you're doing at AlphaGen the meaningful work you were expecting to accomplish?"

"No, not really. In fact, I'm beginning to think it was a mistake. Somehow, using biotech to create fish food isn't exactly Nobel Prize-winning biomedical research. But I guess I'm stuck with it until I find something else."

"And you're thinking shark fins might be what you're looking for?" His skepticism was obvious.

"Maybe. At least it's an interesting diversion that could lead to something."

Ashley looked up the road as police cars and emergency vehicles approached. With light bars ablaze and sirens wailing, they sped past in the direction of the warehouse.

"Wow! That was surprisingly fast for this town. I must have said something right. Let's go back to the docks and watch. From a distance. With the police there, things should be safe."

Clive pulled the Bronco up a few buildings away from the warehouse. The area was crawling with police cars and ambulances, lights flashing. Police cordoned off the area with crime scene tape.

Ashley walked up to a cop who was standing outside the yellow border.

Before she could say anything, the cop held up a hand and said, "I'm sorry, ma'am. This is a crime scene. You'll have to stay clear."

Back in the car, Ashley and Clive watched as ambulances took away corpses in body bags. The CSI unit scurried about, entered the building, and quickly emerged, carrying several small evidence bags.

The routine was broken by rapid-fire squawking from a police radio. An officer reached into a car and pulled out the mike. He listened, talked excitedly, started shouting orders. All the police got into their cars and drove off in a hurry, lights flashing, sirens wailing, followed shortly by the ambulances.

"That was weird," Ashley said.

"What about this isn't?" Clive replied.

"No, I mean they took away the bodies and some evidence bags, but I didn't see anybody carrying those boxes of shark fins. That doesn't make sense."

"Maybe they don't like soup."

"No, really. If this is a crime scene, shouldn't they take all the evidence they can?"

"You could just chalk it up to sloppy police work."

"We have to go have a look," Ashley said.

"You know, I'm beginning to think you have a ghoulish streak."

The two sleuths slipped in through the still-open door, found the light switch and looked around. The warehouse was empty. No bodies, no boxes.

"The fin boxes are gone," Ashley said. "Someone was here after us and took them…before the cops arrived. Someone took them but left the bodies. Someone didn't want the police to find the fins."

"Seems pretty minor compared to all the death and destruction," Clive said. "Someone clearly has a misplaced sense of value."

"Well, I guess the trail has gone cold, for now," Ashley said.

CHAPTER 13

It was pretty late the following Thursday evening, pushing ten o'clock, and Clive was returning from a late-night videogaming session at a friend's. He just happened to cruise past the AlphaGen parking lot, again, despite it being out of the way. And he just happened to notice Ashley's yellow VW in the parking lot, alone except for one other car that he recognized as belonging to Mordecai, another member of the IT crew. He parked next to Mort's Prius and made his way to the IT dungeon.

"Hey, Mort, my man. Did you draw the graveyard shift again?"

Mort quickly closed the screen of his laptop. "Uh. Oh. Hi Clive. Yeah, I'm on the Golden Tilapia deathwatch. Absolutely zilch happening. There's someone in that lab processing samples according to the feed, but I might as well be home asleep, things are running so smoothly, as usual. I don't mind the overtime pay, but it seems like a silly waste of time."

"Tell you what, Mort. I didn't finish updating software in the surveillance system this afternoon. It's the other thing besides the Golden Tilapia project that Roper actually pays attention to. I can do that and monitor Golden Tilapia at the same time, given how smoothly things are going. You can leave and I'll log you out when I'm done, in a couple of hours, around midnight. That should be the end of your shift, right?"

"Hmm," Mort said. "I guess that would work. Are you sure? You've been on graveyard a couple times this week already."

"Seems like my most productive hours, usually uninterrupted. Sleep is way overrated, anyway. I'm happy to do it. You can pay me back sometime."

"Why not?" Mort said. "Thanks, Clive. I owe you."

"No problem at all."

Mort picked up his laptop and barely waved as he left the IT room. Clive settled in and turned on the surveillance feed from the Golden Tilapia lab. Ashley was at her work station, glancing at the readout on a monitor.

"Okay," Clive said to himself. "I'm done just waiting for something to go wrong. I can only blame myself for having designed the system too well. Let's think. A quick, isolated power outage should cause little trouble beyond the need for a system reboot. Which will have to happen in the tilapia lab."

He went to a large circuit breaker panel, found the label for the correct room, and flipped the switch off, then on. And waited.

Thirty seconds passed before the phone rang. He let it ring a couple more times, then said, "IT here, what's the problem?"

"Clive, is that you?" Ashley asked. "Oh good. I don't know what happened, but all the machines went down at once and only some of them have come back on. I was almost finished for the night and now this has happened. Is this something you can handle? I hope."

"Doesn't sound too complicated," Clive replied. "Probably just a matter of reset buttons on the machines that didn't power back up. If you know where they are, you can probably handle it yourself. They're usually on the backs of the instruments."

"Uh, I'm embarrassed to admit that my training stopped at troubleshooting instruments. Something about breaching warranties by doing something a licensed technician was paid to do. Probably just a way to make work for someone else. Am I dead in the water?"

"Naw," Clive said. "As the head of IT, I'm supposedly authorized to fix electronic stuff. And I really suspect it's no more than pushing a button. I'll be there in a jiffy."

"Thank you, Clive. You're a lifesaver," Ashley gushed.

Clive almost blushed. Almost.

He knocked on Ashley's lab door and she let him in. "Show me the patient. Or patients," he said.

Ashley led him to her work station and pointed out two lifeless instruments. He reached around the back of one and pushed a button and it sprang to life. He did the same with the second, with the same positive result. "That should do it," he said, triumphantly.

"Hooray," Ashley exclaimed. She immediately looked at the monitor above the instruments. "Whew, the outage didn't abort the run. This is a time-consuming step in the gene splicing I'm doing. Thank you again. It's good to know you or someone in your room is here monitoring stuff."

"Yeah, Roper's put this project ahead of everything else, enough to pay overtime to extinguish brushfires. I'll just hang out a couple of minutes to make sure the reboot is successful. I'm closer to the action that way. And there's nothing else happening in the IT room." Clive almost felt guilty at his subterfuge.

Ashley smiled and said, "Yes, my lucky night, I guess."

They were silent for a minute or so, then Ashley said, "So, Clive, I've told you my sordid backstory, or at least the parts I'm not too embarrassed to reveal. But what about you? Is riding herd on a building full of electronic illiterates your dream job? And were you always a computer geek?"

"No and yes. I'm hoping AlphaGen is a stopover on my way to Google or Facebook or my own company. And yes, damn straight, I was born to program, right from day one. I built my first computer at eight, sold my first video game at twelve."

"Sounds like you were some kind of prodigy," Ashley said.

"I don't know," Clive responded. "If I was, it was pretty selective, because I was a lousy student. I never graduated from high school, because it was boring. My parents freaked out when I told them I was quitting school. I was only fourteen. They were convinced I'd wind up like so many other dropouts in the 'hood…in jail or dead. My mom broke down in tears and my dad accused me of selling drugs. He said, 'I knew it. That's how you can afford all that computer stuff you have. You sit in your room at night and get high and listen to that awful hiccup music.'"

"He really said that?" Ashley asked.

"Yeh, for real. We hadn't been communicating much I guess. So I said, 'No Dad. The *hip-hop* music helps me concentrate when I'm developing software.' He still didn't get it." "'What's software?' he asked. 'Is that like a hookah pipe?' 'That would probably be considered hardware, Dad,' I told him. 'Software is the computer instructions I write for the video games I sell that lets me buy better computer stuff.'"

Clive sighed, thinking about the different planets he and his parents inhabited.

"I showed them copies of my patent applications, which at least gave them pause. They were still concerned about my not having a high school diploma. I promised to take the GED and apply to college. They felt better when they saw my college entrance exam scores. I got accepted to Caltech and breezed through with a major in artificial intelligence."

"Sounds to me like you were headed for the NSA, or at least NASA," Ashley commented.

"That was a possibility. But I first went commando and started freelancing. Video game software lost its challenge. I guess it was a gateway drug to harder stuff. I used my artificial intelligence background and built an AI-based, augmented reality, interactive, lifelike, child sex robot."

"Yuk! That's disgusting! What are you? Some kind of pervert?" Ashley said, inching away from him.

"No way," Clive said indignantly. "I figured it was better that the perps stayed home and played with my robot than ventured out and chased panties."

"Maybe. Okay, I'll grant you that. Still not exactly the moral high ground. So, what happened?"

"Well, things were cool, and I made a bundle, started my own company that I called Macrosoft. But I ran afoul of the law."

"Lots of potential for that given the cesspool you were playing in."

Clive shrugged. "I guess so, but I was more interested in developing the technology, and porn was a huge market. Low hanging fruit. And things would have been fine, except I built my robot as a prepubescent Hannah Montana lookalike. Hannah's...er, Miley's daddy used his influence, and I got busted for violating her right of publicity, something about name, image, and likeness. The relevant copyright legislation was kind of gray, so they made me dissolve the company and confiscated the assets. I only got three years' probation, sort of a bad conduct discharge. That's when Roper picked me up on a work-release program. I guess he saw some potential."

"I can see where your accomplishments would have appealed to him," the sarcasm in her voice obvious. But she had stopped moving away.

"Aside from that, I think he hired me to avoid the bad optics of ignoring diversity, equity, and inclusion."

"What about Flo and Talulah? Shouldn't Asian American and African American qualify?"

"Roper's not only a universally acknowledged sexist, but also a tone deaf racist," Clive answered matter-of-factly. "Especially when it comes to people he sees as lesser beings. To him they're inconsequential, invisible. Therefore, they don't count."

"So, he's selectively racist?"

"More like he suffers from moral dysphoria," Clive offered.

Ashley nodded, paused. "Whatever it is, it's a big mistake. Flo keeps the lab functional, and Talulah is the collective conscience of the entire building."

Ashley's machine let out a series of beeps. "Finally," she said. "That run's complete, and I'm beat, had it for the night. I really appreciate you coming to my rescue, Clive."

"Glad I could help. Don't hesitate to call," Clive replied.

Clive left Ashley's lab and walked down the hall, humming, "We are the champions…of the world." At the IT room, he sat in his chair, watching the clock. When it struck midnight, he signed Mort out and left.

CHAPTER 14

"OCEAN FESTIVAL DAYS" and "WOUNDED WARRIORS' OPEN WATER CHALLENGE" read the banners above a bandstand, festooned with red, white, and blue bunting. A large, bathing suit-attired crowd milled around, while a KNSX News helicopter hovered overhead. On the stage, an aging, long-haired guitarist gamely plucked out his extraordinary rendition of Jimi Hendrix's "Star Spangled Banner."

As the last strains of the classic died, an overly exuberant male announcer jumped up on the stage and shouted into a mike, despite the speaker feedback. "Awright! Let's hear it long and loud for the Are You Experienced Experience!"

The crowd cheered.

"Thank you all! You guys are fantastic!" he cut in, silencing the assembled mass. "It's finally time for the kick-off event of this weekend's festivities, the Wounded Warriors' Open Water Challenge. Are the swimmers ready?"

All turned and looked at a dozen young men and women in competition swimsuits, waiting by the water's edge. Some were on crutches, others in wheelchairs. All were missing at least a leg. Some wore a prosthesis, others did not. They waved toward the stage. Several kayaks and one canoe sat just offshore, ready to give aid if necessary.

"Okay. Swimmerrrrsss, take your marks…GO!" He fumbled with an air horn that finally emitted a squeak.

Those on crutches tossed them back to assistants and plunged into the water. The wheelchair riders pushed forward into the water and abandoned their chairs. The crowd cheered even louder.

The helicopter dropped down and followed as the group of swimmers headed offshore toward a large red buoy. Paddling in parallel with the competitors were the kayaks and the canoe, the latter manned by two young boys churning the water to stay ahead of the pack.

As the flotilla reached the red buoy, the boys attempted a sharp left turn. The maneuver was sufficiently violent, and the effort so uncoordinated, that the canoe tipped over, dumping the boys into the water, bringing everything to a halt.

The swimmers reached the boys first. Neither boy was wearing a life jacket and, apparently, neither was any more proficient in the water than in the canoe. The swimmers quickly coordinated a rescue, two righting the canoe, entering it, and bailing the water out with their hands and with the paddles. Other swimmers spun the boys around and executed cross-chest carries, returning the boys to the canoe. All swimmers joined in the effort of lifting the boys back into the canoe, just as the kayaks arrived. The race resumed.

Seen from below, the clustered swimmers were, at first, largely obscured by their splashing as the group sprinted toward the buoy. If a viewer approached closer, when the canoe catastrophe unfolded and the swimmers paused, it would have been clear they were all amputees.

In the helicopter following the swimmers, the pilot, copilot, and a videographer hanging out the door strained to watch the unfolding drama, but it was lost in the downblast of the prop wash. Despite wearing headsets, the helicopter occupants still had to shout to be heard.

"Did I see something below the swimmers?" the pilot asked.

"I think I saw something," the copilot answered. "It looked like dark shadows that got larger but then vanished."

"Probably just some seaweed floating in the current," the pilot suggested.

"I guess so," the copilot said. "Hey, Ethan, did you get anything?"

"I was trying, but we were too damn low, so all we're going to see is churned-up water. Let's move to the harbor for the boat parade. And this time, stay higher so I can get some usable footage, okay?"

"Sorry about that. I'm too used to doing freeway traffic reports and police chases. The station insists on dramatic, close-up stuff."

The helicopter banked and headed off into the distance.

Boats of different types, sizes, and colors, as varied as the people on them, paraded along the harbor waterfront, each decorated with strings of flags. The flagging was mostly contemporary American, but a few smaller, funkier boats sported green and yellow Buddhist prayer flags.

The boats proceeded slowly past a viewing stand on one pier, where many of the city's lesser dignitaries and their children waved and cheered, while their dogs barked when not engaged in serious butt sniffing. Above the grandstand, a now-familiar banner declared "OCEAN FESTIVAL DAYS." Below it was another banner proclaiming,

"ANNUAL BLESSING OF THE FLEET." All along the waterfront, the mood and dress were festive, with beach-attired revelers dancing to a variety of local bands. The KNSX News helicopter hovered high overhead.

Decked out in red, white, and blue bunting, the *Stinky Wrinkle* led the parade. Five rows of flags streamed from the back of the *Wrinkle*'s wheelhouse and down to the deck, fanning out to five points on the stern. When viewed up close, "Big Al's Used Cars" could be seen printed on each flag. Captain Agatha Garmin gave an occasional blast on the *Wrinkle*'s foghorn.

The mayor, a priest, and crew chief, Rowdy Wagner, stood on the stern, shouting and waving greetings to the crowd, the priest less enthusiastically than the others. The mayor wore his trademark red cowboy boots and red ten-gallon hat.

The priest stared gloomily at the churning wake behind the boat and said, "Dear Lord, beneath this glassy surface is a world of gliding monsters."

"Huh? Something wrong?" Rowdy asked.

"I hate boats and I hate the water," the priest replied.

"In that case, how come you're here?" Rowdy asked.

"I drew the short straw."

"Your lucky day, too, eh," the mayor said to him. Turning to Rowdy, he added, "You guys could have at least cleaned up some of the fish guts for today, eh? I can see where this boat gets its name."

"So sorry, yer honor. Agatha had us shark fishing all night and we barely made it back in time for this dog and pony show."

"Big Agatha works you guys pretty hard, eh."

"Yeah, we gotta stay numero uno in the fleet so she can lead this parade every year. And I'd be careful how you walk around the boat in those boots. Things could be slippery."

"I wear these everywhere," the mayor replied. "That's what my public expects. And maybe I should think about getting the school board to give the seafood contract to another, cleaner boat."

"And incur the wrath of Agatha. I dunno. I wouldn't—*What the hell?!*"

"*Holy-Jesus-Fucking-Mary-Mother-of-God!*" the priest swore.

"Not again," Rowdy exclaimed.

Finless sharks leapt up over the stern, led by a larger shark with obvious legs where its side fins should be. Another shark held onto her tail and other sharks followed, each holding the stump of the shark ahead.

They attacked the mayor, priest, and crew members, chomping off legs and arms. The mayor tried to escape but slipped and fell, becoming entangled in the flags and bringing the priest down with him. The priest screamed and writhed like a rat caught in a glue trap. Both men were dispatched by sharks.

Rowdy, knowing what to expect, dodged behind the large drum winch.

Agatha rushed to the back of the wheelhouse and surveyed the scene below. The now captainless *Wrinkle* swerved, crashing into the pier with the Annual Blessing sign.

Leaping down from the wheelhouse, Agatha grabbed a fire ax. With it in one hand and her knobby walking stick in the other, she started hacking and bashing sharks. The sharks quickly slipped off the boat, some with arms or legs in their mouths.

Around the harbor, the scene quickly degenerated into bedlam. The boats that were following the *Wrinkle* accelerated in all directions, several crashing into each other or into the docks. Screaming people were everywhere, on the other boats and on shore. Some were screaming while shooting video with their cell phones. The KNSX News helicopter swooped down, Ethan, the videographer, hanging out a door, filming.

Ashley and Clive were on their way back to AlphaGen, listening to monaural classical music on the radio, a compromise given Clive's passion for hip-hop and Ashley's preference for country and western. The music stopped, followed by dead air.

"We interrupt our regularly scheduled programming for a breaking news bulletin. Stan Daily of TV station KNSX is at the municipal boat harbor, where the annual blessing of the fleet festival is underway."

"Pandemonium has gripped our usually peaceful harbor," Daily began. "The scene here is one of absolute catastrophic chaos. Sharks have attacked people on a fishing boat in the boat parade. There appear to be injuries and perhaps fatalities, including, possibly, our beloved mayor. Please stay tuned to this station for further details."

Ashley turned to Clive. "Holy hell. It's happening again. Pull in over there and we'll see if it's on TV."

They turned into the parking lot of Didn't Ask Bar & Grill and rushed inside. It was a typical sports bar, with two walls of TVs and one giant screen. All TVs were tuned to the local news channel, everyone watching the big screen, stunned and silent. Stan Daily was again reporting from a pier overlooking the mayhem.

"...and we just got video feed from the KNSX chopper, taken only minutes ago."

The video played, showing the attack, disarticulated limbs flying around, and Big Agatha's reaction.

"Ooh. That's going to leave a mark," Clive said, as they stood and stared, unbelieving, at the TV.

"Did I imagine it or did one of those sharks have legs?" Ashley asked.

"I don't know," Clive replied. "It all happened so fast. Hard to tell."

"And did you see what that woman did?"

"You mean the fat lady on the boat with the sharks?"

"Yes, that one."

"Yeah. That's one lady with big balls," Clive said.

"Yes. I mean, no. Besides that. I mean she was chopping up sharks, but they didn't seem to care. They just kept biting."

"I don't think that's so weird," Clive said. "I've read that you can slice a shark open, toss it overboard, and it will eat its own guts."

"This was a lot more than slicing them open. She chopped a couple up. It's like they can't die."

"Or maybe they're already dead," Clive said.

"You mean they're like zombies?"

"I don't know, Ashley. Can sharks do that?"

A drunk near them at the bar leaned over and slurred, "Ish tha zhombie sharkopolypsh!"

Ashley grabbed Clive by the arm and pulled him toward the door. "I've got an idea. Let's go."

"Where are we going?" Clive said, more than a little reluctant to move.

"To the harbor," a determined Ashley replied.

"Why the harbor? I'd think *away* from the harbor would be a more prudent direction."

"We've got to find that fishing boat," Ashley said.

"Somehow, I'm not surprised. Well, it shouldn't be too

hard to find. It'll be the one with all the miscellaneous human body parts."

"I'm not interested in the people. I want shark pieces."

"And why's that?" reluctance still evident in Clive's question.

"DNA analysis. I want to compare shark muscle with the fins we took from the warehouse."

"Hey, it's the weekend. Roper doesn't pay me overtime."

CHAPTER 15

The shark with legs and several finless sharks, some carrying human legs and arms in their mouths, approached small but similar sharks. The baby sharks faced the approaching finless adults and became agitated, swimming in tight circles.

The moms bit the arms and legs, tearing them into smaller pieces and then fed them to their ecstatic offspring.

CHAPTER 16

The Bronco slowed as they approached the docks where the fleet blessing and massacre had occurred. Police cars and ambulances were parked haphazardly behind crime scene tape and tangled flagging. Uniforms came and went from the *Stinky Wrinkle*. Ashley and Clive hung back, leaning on Clive's car.

Who should walk up to them but Luke, no limp noticeable.

"Hi, beautiful," Luke said nonchalantly. "Who's your friend?"

Ashley started to take a step back but was stopped by the Bronco. "What? They let you out already? Last time I called, they said you were unconscious and unresponsive. You look pretty responsive right now. That was a miraculous recovery."

"Naw. I really wasn't all that bad off. I kinda like faked the coma thing. They were giving me some awesome drugs, but they stopped, so I snuck out. That oughta slow down the billing. But I saw all the shit on TV and wanted to know what my shark buddies were up to. What are you doing here?"

"Same as you, it looks like. Under less false pretenses. Clive here works with me at AlphaGen. But keep quiet, okay?" She glanced down at Luke's leg. "Do you always wear that thing?"

Luke patted the dive knife strapped to his left leg. "Oh yeah, it's my good luck charm. Saved me from a world of hurt back there. The shark that bit me got hung up, like on the thick plastic sheath, hardly broke the skin. I think most of the blood on my leg was, like, from the other people. Uh, I mean, maybe from the shark's mouth."

Ashley started to say something, then shrugged. "Whatever. Looks like officialdom is leaving. Our turn. Let's make this quick."

When the emergency vehicles had driven off, the three sneaked onto the *Wrinkle*. Clive and Luke stood watch as Ashley picked up shark chunks from the boat's deck. She held them up for a moment, looking around. Finally, reluctantly, she put them in her purse.

"Damn. I knew I shouldn't have splurged on a Balenciaga handbag."

CHAPTER 17

Flo Takata and Vita, a friend from work, pushed a shopping cart through the aisles of an upscale food market. Checking recipes on their cellphones, they scanned the shelves for ingredients.

"Almost done," Vita said. "Two more stops—fish, and some wine to go with it. Whaddya think, red or white?"

"Probably white, I think. I don't know, really. I'm not too good on wines."

The two shoppers walked slowly up and down the wine aisles, picking up bottles, reading the labels, and putting them back in the racks as if they'd burned their fingers.

"They're all so damned expensive," Vita said. "Oh, here's something a little more reasonable." She picked up the bottle and showed the label to Flo. "The price is right. Is this a good year?"

"Well, it has been so far."

"Sold. Okay, Flo. This is where you can shine, the main course. We've got miso soup, sushi-style rice, dried seaweed, soy sauce. That leaves only the fish. What should we get?"

"I, uh, don't have a clue," Flo said, almost in a whisper. "I've never made sushi before."

"What? You're kidding me, of course."

"No, really," Flo answered, almost in tears. "My parents were second generation Japanese American. Their parents had been 'relocated' during World War II and they made a conscious effort to disassociate from anything Japanese, insurance against the next pogrom. All they wanted to do was assimilate. That's why they named me Florence, and my sister Allison, avoiding common or traditional Japanese names. Unfortunate, seeing as how my grandparents couldn't pronounce the letter L."

"Florence isn't a particularly common American name, either," Vita remarked.

"I know. They were still learning. But mainly we never ate traditional dishes. I can make great lasagna, crepes, borscht. But I'm lost when it comes to sushi."

"Ouch!" Vita said. "When we said we'd do the Japanese part for tonight's AlphaGen exotic dinner club, I assumed it would be a slam dunk for you. Why did you agree?"

"Well, uh," Flo whispered. "You seemed so gung ho, and I guess I didn't want to disappoint you. I'm sorry. I..."

"Oh, Flo, there you go again, selling yourself short. It's not a big deal. We'll pull this off. We'll make sure the sushi gets served late, after everyone's had a chance to drink, hopefully in excess. Right now, we have to go fishing."

Their final stop was the seafood counter. Fillets of various fishes lay nestled on beds of shaved ice. The section smelled only slightly of fish.

"I wonder why so many of these fish are always sold as fillets, never whole," Vita asked.

"Maybe because they're all so ugly," Flo offered.

Each fillet was labeled with a price and a country of origin. "Orange Roughy, twenty-two dollars a pound, Product of New Zealand, ouch," Vita read out loud. "Patagonian Toothfish, twenty-eight per pound, Product of Chile, double ouch. 'Bluefin Tuna,' twenty-five dollars, Product of Spain. Wait, here's one. '*New item!* Golden Tilapia,' nine-ninety-five, Product of Norway. Well, going with budgetary considerations over provenance, I'd say the tilapia is an excellent choice, madam."

"I guess so," Flo replied. "But that's strange. I'm working on something called the Golden Tilapia project. We've made some breakthroughs, partial success, to the point that first generation product has been shipped. But I'd swear all our fish came from some supplier in Chinatown. And I didn't think they grew tilapia in Norway. I think they're a tropical fish like from Africa or South America. At least all the tanks in the aquarium room are kept warm. When you walk in there, you immediately start sweating. I wouldn't think they could live in Norway."

"Hey. I'm more concerned with not going broke putting this meal together, given what they pay us at AlphaGen. I say we get the tilapia and let someone else worry about geography."

"Sure. Okay. I guess," Flo acquiesced.

They headed for the checkout counters.

Flo and Vita arrived at the AlphaGen employee's exotic dinner party an hour later. They headed straight for the kitchen with their bags of groceries, stopping only long enough to grab a glass of wine. A dozen people had gathered in a small apartment, the evening hosted by workers employed in various divisions of the AlphaGen empire. Flo refilled her wine glass several times during and after preparing the sushi, which wound up looking almost like the photos on their phones.

"Hey, where's Ashley?" the host asked over the uproar. "Didn't she promise to make some traditional Teutonic dish based on an ancient family recipe?"

"That's right," a member of the Golden Tilapia team answered. "But she's probably back at the lab. She told me she's been working late nights, putting the final touches on the tilapia project."

"I notice boy genius Clive has been only too willing to burn the midnight oil too," Mort, from the IT team added, "even when he's not scheduled. I think there might be something happening there."

"Wow, talk about beauty and the geek," the host replied.

Flo quickly jumped to Ashley's defense, her words a little slurred from her fourth or fifth glass of wine. "Ashley works three times harder than anyone here and makes us all look good as a result. Roper took this project on, pretending it was some sort of breakthrough technology. But it's not. It's really simple gene modification protocols, something Ashley can do with her hands tied. It's not like Roper's pushing back the foreskin of science. I mean—"

Flo stopped, her hand flying to her mouth. The room went silent, everyone surprised at Flo's uncharacteristic outburst, not to mention her word choice. Realizing what she had said, Flo's face turned beet red. After about five seconds, the entire group broke into laughter, then applause.

"Time for the sushi course," Vita announced. "And perhaps a cup of herbal tea for Flo."

CHAPTER 18

"Midnight forensics sounds fascinating, Ashley," Clive said, "but weren't you supposed to go to the international foodfest tonight? I'm sure our coworkers are going to miss you."

The threesome had somehow managed to squeeze into Clive's sister's Bronco, Luke relegated to the back. He climbed onto the saddle and whooped all the way to AlphaGen.

"Oops. You're right, Clive," Ashley said. "I completely forgot about it in the whirlwind of shark attacks. But it's too late now and, anyway, I didn't buy any of the secret ingredients I'd need to put together some Worth-family sauerbraten. The United Nations of cuisine will have to survive with one less country. Plus, if I showed up with Luke in tow, I'd restart the grinding of the rumor mill. They'll be fine without me."

Ashley swiped her card and punched in her access code, gaining admittance into the empty building. Clive and Luke followed her to her lab, where the TV was on, as usual. She booted up several pieces of equipment, put on rubber gloves, and began mixing solutions from bottles with long names on the labels.

"Cool," Luke said. "America's test kitchen and NatGeo chemistry kit."

Ashley ignored him and placed a piece of shark meat and a slice of fin on the lab bench.

"First let's find out what kind of shark we're dealing with. I'll run DNA barcoding trials using the cytochrome c oxidase subunit 1 mitochondrial gene, what everyone calls the COI gene, for identifying species."

"Oooh. Talk science to me, babe," Luke crooned.

Clive rolled his eyes, while Ashley ignored Luke, again, and said, "The international repository GenBank has a huge library of DNA from thousands of species for comparison. It used to take a while, but there's a new rapid turnaround search engine called BLAST. We could get lucky."

Placing a small sample of shark meat in a tube, she added chemicals, inserted the concoction into a machine, pushed buttons, and sat back. After a few minutes, she moved the tubes to a second machine, anticipation on her face. Clive looked on with interest. Luke was bewildered and wandered over to watch a game show on TV.

Minutes later, the machine beeped. Words scrolled across the computer screen next to the machine.

"Bingo! We're in luck! We've got a match, and much faster than even I hoped for. The DNA database says that these are sand tiger sharks."

Clive commandeered a nearby computer, typed in a password. "Let me look at the Wikipedia page on them. Hold on. Cool. They have different names in different countries. They're called gray nurse sharks in Australia and ragged-tooth sharks or raggies in South Africa. They have a scientific name I won't even attempt to pronounce. Strange. They're not supposed to be on the West Coast."

Luke perked up at that and chimed in. "Maybe they emerged from the Marianas Trench after a nuclear explosion."

Neither Ashley nor Clive reacted. Clive continued reading the entry. "It says they're relatively placid and slow-moving, not normally a threat to humans. Boy, did Wikipedia get that one wrong. So much for volunteer fact-checking. And look at the schnoz on these guys! What a set of choppers! I'd call them snaggle toothed, not ragged tooth sharks. I sure wouldn't want to meet one in a dark alley. Or underwater. Or on a boat. Or, God forbid, in a warehouse, for that matter."

Hearing the others mention sharks, a subject more to his liking, Luke returned to look at Clive's computer. "Hey. It says they're the only shark known to burp and fart, because they gulp air at the surface to be buoyant. Woohoo. Farting sharks! Every twelve-year-old boy's fantasy."

"The appeal appears to extend into adulthood, if not maturity," Ashley commented.

Clive and Luke watched as Ashley placed five samples from what she hoped were different sharks in special tubes and shoved them into slots in a machine. After a pause, the machine printed out words and letters on the machine's monitor:

Run 1: ACTGACTGACTGACTGCTGACTGACT-GATGCATGCATGCA
Run 2: ACTGACTGACTGACTGCTGACTGACT-GATGCATGCATGCA
Run 3: ACTGACTGACTGACTGCTGACTGACT-GATGCATGCATGCA
Run 4: ACTGACTGACTGACTGCTGACTGACT-GATGCATGCATGCA
Run 5: ACTGACTGACTGACTGCTGACTGACT-GATGCATGCATGCA
ERROR 429
END

"What's that, babe?" Luke asked.

"Well, I'm running the standard analysis for the 648 base-pair region in the mitochondrial COI gene to see if the sharks are somehow related. Something's weird. Hold on and I'll try different samples."

Ashley repeated the operation and read the output, which was identical to the first five.

"Hmmm. I've run both the shark meat and several fins, and I keep getting the same result, including Error 429. Error 429 means a statistically impossible result. That's because the DNA sequences for all sharks and the shark parts are identical."

"So, you screwed up somewhere," Luke offered.

"No. Or unlikely. I can do these runs in my sleep. The analysis keeps coming out the same. Think about it. From everything we know, all the sharks were females, same size, looked alike, behaved the same."

"Yeah, like they were all multiple amputees."

Ashley ignored Luke. "I think the analysis is right. The likelihood of unrelated individuals having identical DNA fingerprints is like one in a billion. We've got individual sharks with identical mitochondrial DNA, which you only get from your mother. This can only mean one thing. They're clones, females produced asexually by partheno-genesis."

"Say what?" Luke asked.

"I'll spell it out for you, Luke. These sharks didn't have daddies. Mom did it all by herself. They were produced without shark sex."

"Now there's a buzz killer."

Clive glanced up from his computer. "How do you spell prathogenitalia? I'll look it up."

"Just type in p-a-r-t-h and sharks. It'll probably come up," she said.

Clive typed, then paused. "Bingo! Some small sharks in an aquarium in Japan had babies without daddies. And it's also been seen in some other sharks, like…something called a swellshark, and a bamboo shark, and a zebra shark, all in aquaria, so the females didn't have access to mates. So, I guess it *can* happen, at least under certain conditions."

Luke was still peering over Clive's shoulder. "Whoa! What's that thing? A-1 weird."

"It says here it's a sawfish, some kind of shark," Clive said. "They're on the endangered species list. Apparently, they do the Parthenon thing too."

"Cool, but what's that monstro hedge trimmer doodad sticking out of its mouth?"

Both Clive and Luke looked at an image of a large sawfish with its double-edged swordlike snout. Long, sharp, cylindrical teeth ran down either side. Clive googled "sawfish" and a photo of a Polynesian warrior wielding a sword made from a sawfish snout popped up.

"Oh man!" Luke exclaimed. "Could I ever use one of those in Warcraft!"

Clive's eyes lit up. "Horde!"

Luke shouted, "Alliance!"

"Children!" Ashley said, raising her voice. "We've got big problems right here on the third rock from the sun. Can I get your attention?"

"Later, dude."

"You're on, man."

"Finally," an exasperated Ashley said. "Let's think about this. Or at least try. The sharks are identical, and they think and act alike. And, Luke, you said the sharks attacked as if on a signal, like it was coordinated?"

"Hey," offered Luke. "Maybe they communicate by some sort of sharky telepathy."

"Great," Clive said. "So, it's not only night of the living dead sharks, but we're in the village of the damned sharks too?"

"Hey!" Luke said. "How 'bout attack of the shark clones?"

"Why not?" Ashley said. "That would explain a lot. And by being asexual clones, they have greater intelligence—" she looked at Luke, "—because they're not stupefied by a fixation on sex."

"But does that explain why they're attacking in the first place?" asked Clive.

"I've got an idea about that," Ashley said. "Their fins were cut off by fishermen. They attacked fishermen in the bar and then the warehouse workers who had their fins. Each time they attack, they only bite off arms and legs. I think they're 'finning' their victims in retaliation."

"An eye for an eye, a tooth for a tooth, and an arm for a fin?" said Clive.

"Can sharks do that?" Luke asked.

"I think *these* sharks can," Ashley said. "It all seems like part of a pattern."

"It sounds like you think we're dealing with neurodivergent sharks," Clive said.

Mystified by Clive's characterization, Luke was quiet for a moment, but only a moment. "What about my dive trip?"

Ashley looked up from her instrument. "Didn't the attack at that bar on the docks involve Asian fishermen?"

"Yeah," Luke answered. "Bubba dropped by at the hospital while I was rehabilitating. He talked to Big Agatha when she was trolling the docks looking for crew. She said some of her crew were Asian. So?"

"Well, if some of Agatha's fishermen were Asian, and your dive group was Asian, there's a pattern, right?"

"Wow!" Clive said. "Talk about racial profiling."

"Can sharks do that?" Luke asked again.

"And what about the *Stinky Wrinkle* at the boat blessing festival?" Clive asked.

"That one's easy," Ashley answered quickly. "Motive, means, and opportunity. That's the fishing boat that caught them in the first place."

Clive pushed his chair back from the computer and stood up. "Okay. We've got finless zombie lady sharks attacking fishermen who cut off their fins, or at least the sharks are attacking anyone who *looks* like the people who cut off their fins."

"Hey, what about the *Happy Hooker*, that sportfishing boat that was attacked, Miss Einstein?" Luke chimed in. "That doesn't fit your theory."

"First, it's only a hypothesis, although I'm sure the distinction is lost on you. Second, more importantly, the *Hooker* incident shows how special these sharks are. One of them got caught and the others came to her rescue."

"Sharks don't take things personally, Dr. Worth," Clive stated.

"I think these sharks do," she answered.

"And what about the super shark with what you thought were legs?" It was Clive's turn again.

"I've been thinking about that too. I know it's a stretch, but I work on jumping genes. AlphaGen is making genes jump from one fish to another through their food. So maybe, just maybe, one shark ate a person, and the leg genes jumped from her food to her when her body was trying to regenerate fins. She's the leader. She helps her cloned offspring get around on land. Which explains the daisy chain of sharks that attacked both the *Stinky Wrinkle* at the festival and the *Happy Hooker*."

Clive sat back down and spun around to face Ashley. "Like you said, that's a stretch. A really humongous stretch. We're going from science to woo-woo. I'm not sure I'm ready to suspend disbelief that far."

"Say what?" asked Luke.

Clive and Ashley both ignored him.

"But that still doesn't tell us why they were attacking in the first place," Clive said. "Do you think they're just a bunch of vengeful sharks? I think you've seen too many B-grade sharksploitation movies."

"No, it's not simple vengeance," Ashley replied. "I think it all adds up. I think they want their fins back."

"Can sharks do that?" Luke and Clive asked in unison.

"Maybe. Importantly, if I'm right, they keep looking for them, and even found them in that warehouse. But that was on land, which somehow makes it harder for them to retrieve them, out of their element, as it were. They somehow have to find the fins when they're in the water."

All turned their attention to the TV as a news bulletin flashed on the screen.

"This is Stan Daily at City Hall. Interim Mayor Roswell has called an emergency, late night meeting of the city council, following the tragic death of our mayor. He wants the governor to declare a state of emergency and send the National Guard to kill the sharks that are terrorizing our waters. The meeting is open to the public, but Interim Mayor Roswell asked that everyone remain calm."

"Just what we need," Ashley almost snarled. "A statement like that can only cause widespread panic."

"Fer sure," Luke joined in. "The news will spread like wildflowers."

Ashley looked at him sternly, then decided it wasn't time to be the grammar police.

The newscast shifted from Stan Daily to protestors outside City Hall, marching in the glare of spotlights. On one side of the street, people were carrying signs that read: "Kill the Sharks Before They Kill You," "People Over Sharks," "Stop the Slaughter," etc.

On the other side of the street, people wearing PESTO t-shirts had their own signs: "Payback is Hell," "Fishing Hurts," "Stop the Slaughter," etc.

The police broke up an altercation between two opponents bashing each other with their Stop the Slaughter signs.

"Nothing draws a crowd like a crowd," Clive commented.

"We've got to go to that meeting and end this before they do something drastic," Ashley declared.

"Whoa!" Luke protested. "It's a lynch mob and you want us to stick our heads in the noose?"

"Uh, Luke," Clive interjected. "In my circles, we tend to avoid lynching analogies."

"Oh, yeah. Sorry, Clive. I kinda forgot."

"Ashley, I thought you didn't care about sharks," Clive said. "The city council certainly doesn't."

"I've changed my mind. These aren't your run-of-the-mill Captain D's sharks. They're special and deserve special treatment. We need to save them. And we need to talk some sense into the council."

"Surely, you're joking," Clive said.

The three quickly left the lab and headed for the parking lot, Ashley decidedly quicker than the others. They all piled into Clive's car.

CHAPTER 19

Roper's luxury condo was lavishly furnished, with modern art, recessed lighting, and, of course, a large, well-stocked bar. His home office overlooked a night-lit pool. Sitting at a large desk, drink in hand, he engaged in his habitual surveillance of recorded AlphaGen video feeds, looking at today's footage. As usual, most tapes showed no activity, until he got to the one from Ashley's lab. Turning up the volume, he sat back and watched the evening's entertainment. When it was over, and with a sense of self-satisfaction for being a security genius, he toggled to email and typed:

MISS WORTH. IN MY OFFICE FIRST THING MONDAY MORNING!

Roper returned to the live, multi-screen view of the AlphaGen building that played constantly on his monitor. He was about to shut things down when he noticed a slight female figure enter the building, move through a hallway, and open a door labeled "Aquarium Room, Authorized Persons Only."

A nervous Flo walked into the aquarium room, feeling just sober enough to look for answers to nagging questions. The walls were lined with tanks on stainless steel racks, each tank filled with live tilapia. Pumps pumped, airstones bubbled. One rack was labeled "Golden Tilapia, Imported

Controls," another "Golden Tilapia, Genetically Modified, Experimental."

Flo netted a fish from an imported control tank as she talked out loud to herself to overcome her anxiety. She gently placed the fish on a nearby table. "Sorry, little fella. This shouldn't hurt."

Picking up small scissors, she snipped off a piece of fin and placed it in a vial labeled "A, CNTRL." She returned the fish to its tank and repeated the process with a genetically modified fish from an experimental tank, the vial of which she labeled "B, EXPTAL."

Flo left the aquarium room carrying the vials in one hand and a cloth Whole Foods shopping bag in the other. Her image on Roper's monitor moved from one screen to another until she entered Ashley's lab. Retrieving a paper-wrapped package from the shopping bag, she removed a small, yellow-tinged piece of tilapia fillet bought at the upscale market and placed a piece of flesh in an analysis vial labeled "C, MARKET."

"The sushi from these wasn't really all that bad," she said to herself. "Especially with all the other ingredients. But I could have done without the wasabi Vita insisted I try."

At her computer, Flo clicked on the search link in Google Scholar and typed "Country of Origin (COO) test protocols for fish." Several references appeared on the screen. Scrolling through the links, she finally clicked on one, a scientific paper from the "Journal of Seafood Safety" titled "Geographical Fingerprints of Fish Using mtDNA 16S rRNA Analysis." She smiled.

Placing each of the three vials in slots labeled A, B, and C in Ashley's sequencing machine, she typed in "mtDNA 16S rRNA." Lines of code immediately appeared on the screen. Referring to the Methods section of the scientific paper, she typed in several lines of code, followed by "Output: Species, Country of Origin, Run."

LEDs flashed on the sequencing machine and each tube was illuminated brightly, one then another. Flo drummed her fingers on the lab bench impatiently. The machine hummed for around fifteen seconds before text appeared on the screen:

"Sample A, CNTRL: species—Tilapia; COO China"
"Sample B, EXPTAL: species—Tilapia; COO Norway"
"Sample C, MARKET: species—Tilapia; COO Norway."

"I'll be damned. The genmod protocol is working just fine, and enough genes have jumped to fool the analysis into identifying Chinese-origin fish as from Norway. So, Alpha-Gen is selling genetically modified Chinese tilapia to stores that claim to not carry genetically modified foods."

She took out her phone and made a call.

Roper watched the video feed from the lab, his drink untouched. As Flo read the output on the computer screen, he zoomed in and read over her shoulder. "Sonofabitch! This one's going to be fun."

He picked up his cell phone and car keys and headed for the door, punching in numbers on his phone as he left.

CHAPTER 20

Clive's was the only pink and white Bronco in the city hall parking lot. Pickup trucks were definitely dominant, several sporting US flags and assorted right wing propaganda bumper stickers: "My other auto is a 9 mm." "It's not Right or Left, It's Right or Wrong." If the trio had felt uncomfortable before, they felt downright unwelcome now.

They walked around the picketing protestors and into the meeting chamber. The place was packed, standing room only, and the only place to stand was against a wall in the back. Even the people with chairs were standing, many of them shouting at one another and at the council members seated behind tables at the front of the room.

Ashley's phone had been chirping periodically, which she had ignored. She finally reached into her purse and turned it off without looking. Clive's phone buzzed seconds later and he slipped outside, obviously happy to be leaving the room.

Interim Mayor Roswell stood at the front of the room behind a small lectern bearing the city's coat of arms. He was accompanied by a half dozen councilmen seated on either side of him. Everyone's attention was drawn to Stan Daily and a filming crew as they entered and set up a camera and flood lights. Roswell waited until the TV team was clearly ready before trying to gavel things to order.

"Testing, testing."

Feedback buzzed through the room.

"Ahem. Okay? Good. Thank you all for being here on such short notice. Before we begin, I think it's only appropriate that we observe a minute of silence to honor our beloved mayor, who died so tragically."

Roswell removed his hat and bowed his head. Audience members began to stand up. Some were still getting up when Roswell put his hat back on and spoke.

"Thank you all once again. I'm hoping many of you will find the time to attend the funeral services this Tuesday afternoon, 1 o'clock, when our mayor's remains, or what remains of his remains, will be buried at Meadow Lane Memory Gardens. The mayor's wife, er, widow, has requested that, in lieu of flowers, any financial donations be sent to her favorite charity, the Hidden Hills Bridge Club."

He paused a moment and looked solemn, then resumed. "Given the urgency and importance of today's meeting, I think we'll dispense with the Pledge of Allegiance and invocation and get right to the business at hand. I've invited world-renowned shark expert, Professor Hoffman from the Oceanographic Institute, to tell us what science has to say about the bloodthirsty animals that have us under attack."

Professor Hoffman—in his sixties, short, with disheveled white hair, droopy mustache, and wearing an ill-fitting corduroy jacket with leather elbow patches—stepped to the lectern. He had to reach up and pull the mike down to his height. Clearing his throat and glancing around, it was evident he enjoyed the limelight.

"Let me explain in terms even a layman could understand," he began. "What we certainly have here is a group of aberrantly behaving elasmobranchs, or selachians if you want me to disambiguate the terminology. The photos indicate females of a species known as *Carcharias* or *Odontaspis taurus*, or, in common parlance, sand tigers. The South Africans call them raggies because of their rather formidable dentition. They normally do not occur on this coast, another indication of their aberrance. They are characteristically solitary piscivores…fish eaters. By some quirk of dietary disruption or environmental degradation, they have aggregated and, probably, via social facilitation, have switched foraging mode to mammalian hypercarnivory. My considered and considerable professional opinion is that they should be eliminated quickly, by whatever means available."

The crowd cheered. Clive, back in the room now, started scrolling madly on his phone. Luke stood riveted to the proceedings.

Roswell stepped to the mike and raised it back up. "Thank you, Professor Hoffman." Aside to Hoffman, he said in a low voice, "Miss Franklin at the end of the table will give you your consulting fee."

"The proposal before us," continued Roswell to the group, "is to contact the governor and request National Guard action against these killer sharks that are terrorizing our fair city." He turned to the council members. "All in favor?"

The "ayes" were unanimous and enthusiastic, while the crowd erupted into shouts of "Nuke 'em, now" and related, less-family-friendly epithets.

Roswell held up his hand. "Let's do this in a democratic manner, okay? Any opposed?"

Silence.

"Then the motion carries."

"Wait!" Ashley shouted from the back of the room. "I know how to stop the sharks and we don't have to kill them, along with everything else in the sea."

Professor Hoffman quickly stepped back up to the lectern, clearly affronted by having his authority challenged. He had to stand on his tiptoes to reach the mike. "Young lady," he demanded. "What possible rationale can you give for delaying immediate, decisive, professionally recommended action?"

Ashley made her way to the front of the room and spoke directly to the council. "These sharks are parthenogenetic clones," she pleaded in an excited, louder-than-normal voice. "They've been dismembered by shark fishermen. All they want is their fins back."

Hoffman smiled condescendingly, contempt evident on his face. "That's patently absurd. Sand tigers are not known to reproduce parthenogenetically, nor do any sharks possess the neuroanatomy that would render them capable of an emotion such as 'wanting their fins back.' What are your scientific credentials?"

Ashley stopped to think, then said, "I'm a technician at the AlphaGen labs with—"

Her next phrase was drowned out by uproarious, derisive laughter from the audience.

"—a PhD in computational genomics from UC Berkeley."

"Sheer nonsense," Hoffman almost spat.

A burly attendee halfway back in the crowd shouted, "Shut up, lady. This is war, and right now, we're getting our butts kicked."

The crowd erupted with more shouts of "Bomb the bastards" and "Nuke 'em now!"

Clive and Luke waited while Ashley ran the gauntlet

back to them. Halfway, she stopped, turned, and shouted, "This is a huge mistake!"

Her burly adversary, enjoying the attention, poured it on. "Oh, come on, lady. You got to be kidding. We're talking sharks here, hungry fish with tiny brains and big teeth."

Another audience member joined in. "You're just plain nuts. Go back to your kitchen and do some cooking."

A third added, "Yeah, and cook up some shark steaks."

Hoots, hollers, and laughter followed from the crowd.

Ashley was almost out of the room when she stopped and turned around. "Wait!" she shouted. "Don't you think sharks should have rights too?"

Spontaneous synchronization describes how a large group shifts from random, disorganized activity to simultaneous, coordinated action. Think of an audience bursting into thunderous applause. This is what happened following Ashley's question. Her plea was first met with total silence. Then, after perhaps the count of five, the entire meeting let out a simultaneous, synchronized, derisive guffaw.

Ashley fled the room, followed thirty seconds later by Luke and Clive, who were trying to slip out unnoticed.

Interim Mayor Roswell regained the mike. "It's unanimous. Thank you all for your courageous action during these trying times. I'll make the call immediately. And once the governor gives the Guard the green light, we'll put out a press release so the public knows we are working diligently on their behalf."

Captain Lewmar, of *Happy Hooker* fame, was in the crowd, watching the proceedings. He finally stood up and cleared his throat. Well known by many, and generally respected, his presence silenced the crowd. He didn't even have to go to a blackboard and scrape his fingernails to get attention.

"You better warn people not to go hunting these damn monsters on their own," he said in a commanding voice. "Trust me. They don't die easy."

"Thank you, Captain Lewmar. We'll take that under advisement," Interim Mayor Roswell said. "In which case, meeting adjourned."

Out in the parking lot, Ashley was on the verge of tears. It didn't help that neither Clive nor Luke made eye contact with her.

"I guess it's over," she said among sniffles. "We can't fight Roper, City Hall, *and* the National Guard. I should have never started this stupid thing. I'm a lab tech, not a crusader. Clive, can you please just take me home."

"Hey, wait a minute. You're quitting!?" Clive protested. "Just like that? After all you've found and what we've gone through for you and what you've been saying, you're going to let these dimwits stomp on you a little and toss in the towel? You've got to be kidding!"

"Well, it does seem kind of hopeless, don't you think? Luke, don't you think it's hopeless?"

"Well, there are an awful lot of those dudes, and they're, like, going to call in the army and start bombing, and that doctor guy seemed pretty sure of himself and—"

"Who? Dr. Bluster?" Clive jumped in. "He's a quack, no doubt about it. A fraud, a charlatan, a huckster. He was spouting bullshit so deep I had to pull my trousers up. I was immediately suspicious, so I googled him and found the only paper he's ever published. It was in a scientific magazine called *The American Naturalist*."

"Hey, aren't those nudists?" Luke asked.

"No, Luke. Those are naturists," Ashley quickly replied. "What was it about, Clive?"

"The title of the paper, which looked like it's all speculation, was 'Radio Transmission and Reception Functions of Shark Dorsal Fins.' Here's what the summary said: 'Many sharks swim near the surface, protruding the first and sometimes second dorsal fin above the water's surface. The function of this apparent incidental exposure of the dorsal fin(s) remains unknown. We…' royal we, I guess, since he's the only author, '…propose that the first dorsal fin transmits and second fin receives radio transmissions.'"

"Wow," Ashley exclaimed. "That's patently absurd."

"But wait," Clive cut in. "There's more. The hits just keep on coming. You have to hear his conclusion."

Clive scrolled down on his cellphone. "'One intriguing hypothesis is that sharks, as with life in general, originated extraterrestrially. Are sharks communicating with ancestral life forms that live in other worlds, the theoretical basis of the Search for Extraterrestrial Intelligence (SETI)?'"

"Cool," Luke said. "Sharks are from outer space. Would that make them legal or illegal aliens?"

Clive and Ashley ignored him.

Clive went on. "The article is full of equations and graphs, but from what I got, there's no data. He made it all up. And that's apparently what makes him a self-proclaimed expert on sharks and, coincidentally, shark fins."

"I take it back," Ashley said. "That's not just absurd, it's irresponsibly bad science."

"Absolutely," Clive said. "See what I mean. He's used to people bowing down before his academic robes. Seen it before. No, we've got the data and the high moral ground. Let's keep going."

"Really?"

"Yes, really."

Ashley blew her nose and straightened her shoulders. "Yes, you're right, dammit. We've got to do something before these nutcases wipe out everything in the ocean."

"Atta girl, but we don't have much time. That mayor guy is going to call the governor. Even with the normal inefficiency of the government, the National Guard might be moving in a couple of days. What do you have in mind?"

"Well," Ashley said. "I already had something of an idea, but it's kind of dangerous."

"Why am I not surprised?" Clive said.

"Hey!" Luke said. "I'm on doctor's orders to take it easy."

"Which you're all of a sudden following? I guess it's just Clive and me."

"You and who?" Clive asked.

Ashley turned and looked Clive straight in the eyes. "Fine, Mr. Computer Nerd. In that case, I'll go it alone."

"I was just kidding," Clive said, maybe a tad too slowly.

Luke was next to suffer under Ashley's gaze. "What the hell. Me too, I guess," he offered. "But is it just us? Like, I mean, don't we need more people?"

Clive responded, "For God so loved the world, He didn't send a committee."

Luke hesitated, "Huh? Okay. I get it. So, what is it *we're* going to do?"

Ashley started talking, faster and faster. Soon she was waving her arms. Clive and Luke listened, shaking their heads, faster and faster.

"Whoa! Hold on," Clive finally said. "What you're suggesting is like playing trick or treat at Death's door."

"Those guys were right," Luke added. "You are just plain

nuts. We could get killed. Death isn't, like, something to be taken lightly. At least not my death."

Ashley gave him a very stern look, shook her head and said, "Wuss."

"Oh well, like I said, what the hell"

"Thank you, Luke. It's our only hope. The shoreline is going to be a bloodbath otherwise."

"But how do we find the bad guys?" Clive asked.

"By going back to the warehouse where this all started. I'm guessing that's their base of operations."

With a destination agreed upon, the three headed for Clive's car, Luke in the lead. He climbed into the back area and assumed his preferred post on the saddle. Ashley and Clive were about to get in the front when Ashley's phone chirped. She took it out of her purse and looked at the screen.

"Damn. It's an email from Roper. Double damn. He wants to see me first thing Monday. This can't be good."

"Maybe, maybe not," Clive said. "I had an interesting phone call from Flo, while the mayor was on his irrationally exuberant rant. She apparently couldn't reach you, so she called me."

"Oops. I see I missed several calls from her. I was too wrapped up in trying to reason with the shark vigilantes in there. What's this all about?"

"It's more than a little complicated," Clive said. "I think it will make sense if we go to my place and I show you, before you take us fishing again."

"Can't you just tell me?" Ashley asked.

"I think it's important you see for yourself. Luke can come along, if you're worried he'll be jealous."

"Luke? We're not really, or not anymore anyway. Probably never should have been." She stopped a moment and thought. "What was once a relationship is now like a situationship. He's more of a project. I guess he always has been. And sometimes he's actually helpful, under careful supervision."

CHAPTER 21

Two young boys in a canoe—the same two who had capsized the same canoe during the Wounded Warriors' swim race—were fishing in the dark, near the commercial docks.

Charlie, the younger and smaller of the two, said through chattering teeth, "I'm tired and cold and scared, Jenks. It's really late. Let's stop, before we get in trouble."

"Don't worry, Chuck. Everyone's at that meeting. Think how cool it would be if we caught one of those sharks."

"I'm thinking how uncool it's going to be when my mom finds out we used her lamb chops for shark bait."

"Hey, you're gonna bring home shark steaks instead. Come and get it, sharkee!"

"Can't we just go home?" Charlie pleaded.

The canoe lurched sideways as Charlie's fishing rod was almost jerked out of his hands. He forgot his troubles and started cranking.

"Wow! I bet I got a great white! It must be huge!"

Jenkins grabbed a long-handled net. "Reel it close and I'll land it."

Jenkins reached overboard with the net and, after several failed attempts, scooped up a small shark, obviously a youngster of the same type as the finless females. The little shark fell into the bottom of the canoe, between the two boys. It bounced and thrashed and snapped. Jenkins grabbed a small baseball bat and whacked at it, hitting everything but the shark. He finally succeeded and the shark lay still.

"Aw, it's just a baby," Charlie said. "We caught *a* shark, but not *the* shark. I don't think this is what's been eating people. Do you?"

"Naw. But let's cut it open and see what's inside."

With a kitchen knife also borrowed from Charlie's mom, and after several failed attempts, Jenkins slit the belly open. A large red object slid out. Charlie stood up to get a better look. Neither boy noticed dark shapes swirling in the water around them.

"Holy moly! Is that a cowboy boot?" Charlie exclaimed.

"Or at least part of one," Jenkins said. "And yuk! I think there's still a leg inside it!"

Something crashed into the canoe with a pronounced thud. The boat shuddered violently and Charlie, still standing, tumbled headfirst into the water. He splashed toward the boat and grabbed the gunnel, gasping and crying.

Dark shapes turned and moved toward him.

"Give me your hand, Chuck! Please give me your hand!"

"I can't get up! I can't!"

"Give me your hand, dammit!"

As Jenkins managed to pull Charlie into the boat, the gutted shark sprang to life, thrashing and beating its tail against the sides of the canoe, squirting blood all over. Then, it finally lay still.

Both boys kneeled in the bottom of the canoe, panting, Jenkins shaking, and Charlie sobbing.

Jenkins finally said, "Hey! Don't look at me. You're the one who caught it."

Charlie answered between sobs, "Can we please go home now?"

CHAPTER 22

"Hey, Clive," Ashley commented, "you're something of a minimalist when it comes to decorating."

Ashley and Luke glanced around Clive's living room while Clive booted up his computer on the big screen.

"Just the simple bare necessities," Clive responded, without looking up from his computer. "My feng shui consultant assures me the TV balances the couch, because the energy flows from one to the other."

Luke was clearly puzzled by the exchange but joined in anyway. Stifling a yawn, he commented, "Awesome crib, dude. I love the *Deathly Hallows* cut-out. But who's the dork on the right?"

Ashley shook her head. "Brilliant, Luke. Absolutely brilliant."

Clive was tapping keys furiously, scrolling through pages. Eventually, the Gmail logo popped up and Clive entered, "Username," "DWRoper," "Password," "TheRope."

"Hey, isn't that Roper's account?" Ashley asked.

"Yeah, deeply encrypted. Not exactly the nuclear launch codes. At least it wasn't the Spaceball Syndrome 1-2-3-4-5. It only took a couple of nanoseconds to break in, which isn't surprising, given I created the system. I've hacked in to all his accounts, including his video feeds in his office and condo from the various surveillance cameras around AlphaGen."

"Including the one in the ladies' restroom?" Ashley asked indignantly.

Clive hesitated, then said, "I didn't do it, nobody saw me do it, nobody can prove anything."

"That's hardly plausible deniability. No free passes." Ashley's tone was chilly.

"Regardless," Clive forged ahead. "I like to peek occasionally into Roper's email. It's always good to know what your boss is up to."

"You can read other people's email?" Luke gushed. "That's radical, man."

"No, it's usually pretty boring. But with a sleazeball like Roper, it pays to know what he's thinking before *he* knows what he's thinking. That way I can mount an anticipatory counterattack when necessary. And every now and then, you get lucky."

Clive scrolled back through many emails, finally stopped, hit a few keys, and an instant messaging window popped up.

"I've developed a text-to-voice recognition and dictation program. It lets you listen to instant messaging. I wanted you to hear this little exchange between Roper and a guy named Chang. I've kind of played with their voices."

An instant message appeared on the screen, each line spoken as if the two messengers were talking to one another. Both had the usual monotone cadence of computer-generated speech, but Chang's voice had a Chinese inflection and Roper's sounded like he'd been inhaling helium.

CHANG: "Okay, Roper. We're having trouble moving these fish. What's the chance you can mask country of origin so no one knows they're from China?"

ROPER: "Should be straightforward gene splicing."

Ashley started to giggle and Clive glanced at her sharply. "Sorry," she apologized. "His voice is just too funny. Love it. I'll try to control myself."

"May we continue?" Clive said sternly.

ROPER: "We'll find the right gene from somewhere else, another fish probably, from a country everyone respects, splice it into standard bacteria, work it into the food chain. Get the genes to jump to your fish."

CHANG: "So this is something your technology can do?"

ROPER: "No question. I've got a gorgeous tech who's an expert at it and is hot to advance her career. She'll do anything I ask. Well, just about anything."

CHANG: "Can she be trusted?"

ROPER: "No problem. I'll tell her it will increase growth rate, like they do with genetically modified salmon, providing cheap protein for the starving masses. She's idealistic enough to swallow that. She doesn't have to know the real reason."

CHANG: "Do it."

ROPER: "I'll get her on it. I sure wish I could get on her."

"Wait a second," Ashley said. "Is this what I think it is?"

"Yup, 'fraid so. I did some more digging, or rather, Flo did some digging. She's really sharp, and Roper doesn't pay much attention to her unless he needs a punching bag."

"Flo's a real diamond in the rough."

"Yes, I agree, one hundred percent. I got a phone call from her during our interaction with the enraged citizenry. She explained it all to me. She researched country of origin assays and ran them on some AlphaGen tilapia fillets. Bingo! They came up as being from Norway. So, connecting the dots, it looks like your Golden Tilapia project is bankrolled by someone named Chang, and you're disguising Chinese fish, making them test like they came from Norway. My guess is you're developing a food to give to Chinese tilapia that changes their genes so they won't look like they're Chinese."

"Cool," Luke said. "Nobody wants to eat anything from China."

"That bastard!" Ashley almost spat the words out. "Screw him if he thinks he can use me to do his dirty work, disguising his greedy motives as something beneficial while dangling career advancement in front of me like a fat worm on a hook. I've been acting like an idiot, but this changes everything."

"I thought it might."

"What you've shown me really pisses me off. That bastard!"

CHAPTER 23

As Flo hurried out of the AlphaGen building, she was confronted by a raging Roper.

"Takata!" he shouted. "What were you doing in the aquarium room? That is a sensitive, restricted area, accessed only by my veterinary people. You are not authorized to be in there."

"But, Mr. Roper, sir. I-I don't go in there. All my work is in the sequencing lab."

"Bullshit! You're a terrible liar, Takata. I checked the security database, and it clearly shows you were in there. You could have easily jeopardized the efforts of the whole team. Competent people, unlike yourself. I've had enough! You're fired! Get out!"

Flo stood there with her mouth open, then burst into tears. Clutching her purse, she ran sobbing from the building.

Tear-blinded, Flo stumbled through the darkened AlphaGen parking lot. With shaking hands, she got into her older Honda Civic and managed to get the key into the ignition. Too upset to bother with the seat belt, she raced out of the parking lot, oblivious to a dark sedan idling on the other side of the lot, with its lights turned off. It pulled out seconds later and followed her.

Flo drove too fast at first, then slowed as she tried to regain her composure. She took assurance from her purse on the passenger seat, gave it a pat, took a deep breath, and smiled. Finally realizing she hadn't fastened her seat belt, she twisted to her left to grab the buckle. As she did, she saw the dark sedan pulling up alongside.

At that moment, both cars entered a sharp left curve, clearly marked by a black-on-yellow curved traffic arrow attached to a large oak tree, reflected in their headlights

The dark sedan swerved into Flo, forcing her to the road edge, straight toward the tree. Flo tried to turn her car back to the left, but the sedan had her blocked. She fought, turning the Honda hard into the larger car, with minimal effect other than crunching metal and plastic.

A squirrel, awakened by all the commotion, streaked out from the left and stopped in front of Flo, frozen in her headlights. She swerved right to avoid it, lost control, and slammed into the tree. The impact drove her head into the windshield, her faulty, recalled, Takata (no relation) airbag failing to deploy. The Honda wound up on its side, wheels spinning.

The dark sedan sped away.

The squirrel ran up the oak tree, stopped, then ran back down and began gathering acorns shaken loose by the impact. Seize the moment.

CHAPTER 24

The faded pink-and-white tinge of the Bronco was hardly noticeable in the dark, where Ashley, Clive, and Luke were staked out, across the street from the now-familiar warehouse. Luke took out his phone and started playing a video game.

"Luke, can you shield the light from that damn thing so no one notices us? Please."

"Whatcha playing, Luke?" Clive asked.

"It's called *Honor in Combat*. I just got the latest version, H-I-C 4. Ever heard of it?"

"Heard of it? I wrote the first version back at Caltech when I was a freshman. The publisher ripped me off and I never got royalties."

"No shit! That's amazing. Really?"

"Yeah, really. What about you, Luke? Where'd you go to school?"

"Santa Monica High."

"You're like those pro football players on Sunday night doing their introductions. I meant college."

"Oh, yeah. Kinda skipped that part."

"Right," Ashley laughed. "College can be so oppressive these days."

Luke, clearly missing the dig, said, "Hey. I wanted to be an astronaut, but I found out scuba instructors don't have to take drug tests. Plus, it was a great way to meet chicks. Hey, look at that!"

A Happy Charlie Seafood truck approached the warehouse, headlights off. It backed up to the loading dock, no backup bell sounding, and workers rushed out, carrying three foam boxes. A security light nearby provided enough illumination to show that the boxes they were loading into the truck were labeled "Flounder Fillets."

"Hey, aren't those the same boxes?" Luke mumbled.

"Hush!" Ashley whispered. "We guessed right. It looks like they've managed to recruit a bunch more workers to replace all the ones that were killed by the sharks. You couldn't pay me enough to take on that job, given the obvious risks."

"It's amazing the details people leave out of a job description," Clive said.

The truck left the loading bay and headed down the street, again without headlights.

"Follow them, Clive," Ashley whispered. "Stay back and turn off your damn headlights, for Pete's sake."

"I have a bad feeling about this," Clive replied, and slowly crept out of their hiding place.

Following the truck was difficult, given it was only visible when it braked. It took a twisting route from the harbor, traveling down back roads until it finally merged onto the freeway.

"Do you mind if I turn my lights on now?" Clive asked as they sped up.

"I guess not. But stay back. Try to keep one car between us and the truck. Just make sure you don't lose it."

"Don't tempt me."

After about a half hour, the truck entered the outskirts of a city, and slowed as it approached a freeway sign that read, "Chinatown, next exit." It took the off-ramp, followed by Clive, et al.

"Damn, they didn't even signal they were getting off," Clive complained.

"Given how much of what they're doing is illegal, I'd say that's a minor infraction," Ashley remarked.

After maneuvering through more twists and turns and backroads, the truck turned down a dead-end street lined with old warehouses. It backed up to one that lacked any signs or even a street number. A roll-down door opened, and the truck backed inside.

"Park here," Ashley instructed, pointing to an alley about a block away. "Back in so we can make a quick getaway. We'll watch and see what happens."

"Okay. We found their place," Luke said. "Why don't we just call the cops? Isn't what these guys are doing illegal?"

"No dammit. Think about it. First, we don't know what's really in those boxes. We think they're shark fins, but they could be flounder fillets. Second, if the cops come and find fins, they'll confiscate them as evidence, slap a small fine on someone, and we won't get them back in time to complete my plan. Assuming we can trust the cops."

"You weren't kidding about stealing the fins, were you?" Clive said, more a statement than a question.

"Of course not. That's the whole point."

"No wonder I took up hacking. It's safer."

"So now what?" Luke asked.

"We wait, then we go in."

"Hey. I'm on doctor's orders to take it easy. Really."

After about twenty minutes, the warehouse door rolled back up, the truck left, and the door rolled back down.

"That took longer than I expected," Ashley said, "given

they only unloaded three boxes. They must have unloaded some other stuff. We need to find out. And I don't have to remind you to keep quiet."

They circled the building, trying all the doors, only to find them locked.

"Looks like the end of the line," Clive said.

"Nonsense," Ashley retorted and pointed to Luke's dive knife. "Gimme that thing."

"Whoa, babe. That's not a toy," Luke said, as he reluctantly handed over his prize possession.

"Even better."

Ashley took the knife and quickly jimmied the lock on a door. Pulling it very slowly, it opened, its hinges creaking. She handed the knife back to Luke and quipped, "As Mr. Natural says, 'Always use the right tool for the job.'"

"Wow!" Clive remarked. "I guess that's what happens when you buy locks made in Cambodian daycare centers."

With Ashley leading, they slipped inside, the air of the darkened warehouse stale. Ashley turned on her cellphone flashlight and swept the beam around. It briefly illuminated a rectangular sign on the wall with bold, black, script lettering.

"That's a nice sentiment," Luke said.

"What?" Ashley asked.

"The sign says, 'In God we trust.'"

"Not quite," Clive interjected. "Read it again."

Ashley played the beam on the sign.

"You're right. They crossed out the "od" in "God" and replaced it with "lock. What does that mean?"

"In *Glock* we trust," Clive answered.

"Oh," Luke replied. "Maybe they're not so friendly after all."

"Like, duh," Ashley commented.

Despite moving slowly and carefully in the darkness, they bumped into a table.

"Ow!" complained Luke.

"Hush!" Ashley ordered.

Sweeping her light back and forth, the beam fell across three boxes on top of the table, each labeled "Flounder Fillets."

"Luke! Quick!" Ashley whispered. "Let me see your tool."

"Ooh, Ashley. Is this really a good time?"

"In another universe. Your dive knife, doofus."

Luke reluctantly handed the knife to Ashley, who sliced a box open. Lifting the lid and shining the light in, they discovered…shark fins.

"Bingo!" Clive said.

"Gawd, these things stink," Luke remarked. "They smell like old piss. People actually eat them?"

"Hey, there's no disputing taste, even bad taste," Clive said.

"Shhhh!"

In the semi-darkness at the edge of Ashley's flashlight beam, Luke spied a large, long object leaning against the table. Picking it up, he recognized it as a four-foot-long sawfish snout, with all its protruding teeth, like on the wiki page.

In his excitement, he didn't notice a wire running from the sawfish snout down to the floor. He lifted the snout over his head in both hands and proclaimed, "Ancient spirits of evil, transform this decayed form to…uh-oh!"

The entire inside of the warehouse erupted in buzzing alarms and flashing strobes as the overhead lighting came on. From the depths of the warehouse, barking dogs came charging at full speed toward the intruders.

"Oh shit!" Ashley shouted over the din. "Everyone, grab a box and run."

"Feets, do your stuff," Clive shouted, close on Ashley's heels.

At first, the dogs didn't seem that large, although exceptionally loud for their apparent size. It quickly became all too clear that the three invaders were seeing only the heads of very large animals. Luke picked up a box in one hand and the sawfish snout in the other. Unfortunately, his prize was still attached by the trip wire. Reluctantly, he dropped the sawfish snout and ran.

They got to the door just as the dogs caught up, teeth bared. With their backs against the door, they faced their assailants, waiting for the attack.

Ashley hesitated, then reached into her box and took out a fin, looked at it, hesitated again, then threw it at the snarling canines.

The dogs stopped short, sniffed the air, whimpered, then turned tail and slinked away.

The three intruders rushed outside and leaned against Clive's car, panting.

"Fast thinking, girl!" Clive said when he'd caught his breath. "How did you know that would work?"

"I didn't. But I remembered reading that the best shark repellant was dead shark. I just hoped it would be a dog repellant too."

"I guess that's why you have a P-H-D and I don't," Luke said.

"Only one of many reasons."

"Enough talk," Clive interrupted. "Let's get the hell out of here. Those dogs may have aroused someone with a less sensitive nose."

They tossed the boxes into the Bronco's storage area, on top of the equestrian ropes and harnesses. As Clive closed the liftgate, the boxes pulsated, unnoticed by the car's soon-to-be occupants.

Clive drove away slowly, headlights off.

Parked outside Clive's apartment a half hour later, the three discussed their next move.

"Now what?" Luke asked.

"This is where you come in, Luke. Can you get us a boat and dive gear?"

"Well, I dunno. *Calypso* got impounded after our little incident," Luke replied.

"Incident!" Ashley exploded. "Some incident. You got a boatload of tourists killed."

"Hey. *I* almost got killed."

"False equivalency, Luke. You're alive and they're not. Redeem yourself, find us a boat."

"Hmm," Luke responded. "Maybe I can do something. Security on the dock's been a little loosey-goosey over the past coupla weeks, 'cause everybody's gone to work on the *Wrinkle*. I can probably liberate *Calypso*. It might take a day or so. But there should be enough gear on board, minus what's still on the bottom in the reserve."

"Great. Okay, this is where the other part happens. Clive, can you work some more electronic wizardry?"

"Shouldn't be a problem," he answered. "I've got everything I need at home. But it might take a day for me too. One thing though. I can't scuba. In fact, I can't swim. I took computer programming instead of PE. Actually, I kind of hacked my school records and passed PE without attending."

"No way!" Luke exclaimed, his admiration obvious.

"Yes, way. Hey, I wasn't greedy. I could have given myself an A but settled for a C. Seemed more believable."

"Enough. See you both at the boat at 0600 on Monday, before the world is awake. I'm going to the lab. I want to see if I can scramble the Norwegian fish DNA code and throw a monkey wrench into Roper's holy tilapia project."

"Wow," Clive exclaimed. "When you change stripes, you go Technicolor. But first, I've got to get this car back to my sister. Can I get rid of these stinky fins, so she doesn't have a hissy fit?"

"Sure. That's understandable. Let's take Luke to the harbor, then drop me and the fins off at my place. I'll store them there for safe keeping."

"Okay, mon capitan," Luke said. "We attack at dawn, or preferably a little later."

"I hope it's us who's attacking and not the sharks," Clive commented.

After dropping Luke off, Clive insisted they drive with the windows open "to get rid of some of the smell."

Parked outside Ashley's apartment, the two started to transfer the three boxes of shark fins from the Bronco to Ashley's Beetle.

"You know, Clive, we don't know how many fins we managed to rescue. Let's open things up and count."

Clive raised the lid on two boxes, Ashley dealing with the remaining, heavier box.

"I've got thirteen fins in here," she said. "How many in yours?"

Clive had his back to Ashley and was mumbling to himself. Ashley peered over his shoulder.

"Clive! Are you counting on your fingers?"

"Uh. No. Er. I was picking at a hangnail."

"No, you weren't! You were counting on your fingers. I saw you. Admit it. You don't know how to add."

"Or subtract for that matter," Clive said. "I sort of suffered from a kind of dyslexia through grade school. One of the reasons I didn't graduate was that I always failed math and they kept holding me back as 'cognitively challenged.'"

"But you're a mathematical genius. I mean, look at your fantastic programming skills."

"Math is easy. Give me five simultaneous differential equations, and I can solve them in my head. It's arithmetic that's my Achilles heel. But now that you know, I'll have to kill you."

"That will have to wait for later. Luke needs a dive partner," she said. "Just move over and let me do the heavy lifting, okay?"

CHAPTER 25

On her way to AlphaGen, Ashley's phone chirped from inside her handbag. She removed it, switched to speaker. Looking at the screen, she didn't recognize the number. "Uh, hello?"

"Ashley, it's Talulah, from work. Did you hear about Flo?"

"No! Oh my god! What happened? Is she alright?"

"Barely. Roper lit into her again. Some nonsense about fish in the aquarium room. He fired her on the spot. She ran out crying, got into her car, and must have lost control. She hit a tree. Totaled her car. She's in ICU at Mercy. I just came from there. She's in a bad way, but really wants to talk to you. Said it was important."

"Okay. I was headed for the lab, but I'll go there first. I wonder what this is all about."

"She said you'd understand. Or at least that's what I think I heard through all her bandages."

At Mercy Hospital, Ashley went straight to the ICU desk. Not surprisingly, things were pretty quiet, no nurses on the floor.

"I'd like to see one of your patients, a Ms. Florence Takata."

The receptionist looked at a computer screen. "Her condition's critical. Visiting is limited, especially at this hour. What's your name?"

"Ashley Worth. I got a phone call that she wanted to see me."

"Hmmm. Right. You're okayed, which is surprising, since you're not related. But please be quick and don't upset her. She's hanging by a thread. Room 108."

Checking numbers as she walked quietly down the hall, Ashley found Flo's room. When no one answered her knock, she pushed the door open slowly. Flo was bandaged from head to toe, in traction, tubes running all over, monitors beeping.

"Oh, Flo! Oh, you poor thing! What happened?"

Flo struggled to whisper. "I-I think Roper tried to kill me."

Ashley leaned down to hear better. "Oh my god, you're kidding. Why?"

"He's faking the tilapia assays. I found out." Flo paused, gasped. "It's clearly illegal. He knows I'm on to him. He tried to throw me off, then sent a guy after me." Another pause. "There's a flash drive in my purse…data from your work…my analysis. Take to police."

Flo fell silent, shuddered. Her eyes glazed over but remained open, staring into space. The intermittent beep on a bedside machine turned to a shrill alarm.

"Flo! *Flo!* Oh no! *Nurse!*"

Ashley fumbled with the call button, mashed it. A nurse rushed in, looked at the monitors and Flo, shook her head, made the sign of the cross, and covered Flo with the sheet.

"Oh, Flo. Damn it all to hell. Together, we're going to scorch that bastard. Starting right now."

Driving with tears in her eyes and determination, Ashley parked near the AlphaGen building entrance and walked quickly to the front door. She inserted her pass key into the keypad slot and punched in numbers. The door unlocked, but her card was swallowed by the keypad. Shrugging, she walked inside.

The building was deserted, the halls dimly lit, all the lab rooms dark and silent. As she approached her lab, she encountered Kimo, the night custodian, pushing his broad dust mop along the hallway. Ashley was on a first-name basis with Kimo, in part because no one knew his last name. But Ashley's grad school advisor—a woman admired for her scientific achievements as well as for her treatment of those around her—told Ashley to always give custodians and secretaries the respect they deserved. Although in a hurry, she stopped and asked Kimo how he was doing.

"I'm fine, Ashley," Kimo said in the accented English that Ashley assumed was Hawaiian, partly because Kimo wore a carved bone fishhook around his neck that reminded her of the Disney movie *Moana*.

"You did good tonight, Ashley," he added.

"Huh?"

"I watched you on the television at that meeting," he said. "You stood up for the sharks, against all those ignorant, self-important shark haters."

"Uh, thank you, Kimo. I'm glad you think that way. Not many folks seem to agree with me."

"That's because they have lost touch with nature," he said. "In my family, sharks—we call them *mano*—are treated with reverence. Where we come from, the island of Kaua'i, our legends go back to a time when we had ancestral shark spirits or *'aumakua*. To kill a shark was *kapu*, forbidden. We have many legends about *mano*. One of our *'aumakua* was a tiger shark named Kawelo, who lived at the mouth of the sacred Wailua River. That was a place we often fished. But Kawelo sometimes objected to the intrusion and would eat a trespasser. No one ever thought of trying to kill or capture him. You have that same attitude. You are right and they are wrong."

Kimo went back to pushing his dust mop down the hall.

More than a little puzzled, but buoyed somewhat by the interaction with Kimo, Ashley returned to the more immediate task at hand. At the door of her lab, she punched the usual code numbers on the keypad. The door opened, then closed behind her with an audible, jarring, locking sound that stopped her.

Upon trying the closed door, she found it was locked, apparently from the outside.

It didn't matter. She was a woman on a mission. At her workstation, log-in seemed to go as usual. Getting to work, she positioned herself so as to block the surveillance camera's view of her monitor.

After a few more key entries, the heading on the screen read, "Norwegian Poutfish Genomics" and lines of DNA code scrolled across the screen:

ACTGCTGAATTGACTGTTGACTGTACCT-
GAATGCATGCAT TACCTGAACTAGAC-
TAGACCTTGCTGGACATGATCTGGCA
CTGAATGACATGACGTGCTCGACTTGAA-
CATGATCGCTAT

"Let's see," she said to herself. "Switching a couple of bases should do the trick."

Moving the cursor to the middle of the first line, Ashley typed AGTC where ACTG should have been. She hit return.

The screen immediately went blank. "UNAUTHORIZED USER, ACCESS DENIED" appeared in bold.

"What the fu—"

Roper's voice erupted from the intercom speaker. "Miss Worth! Just what do you think you're doing?"

Startled, Ashley turned and faced the surveillance camera. "Uh, um, hello, Mr. Roper. Just trying to catch up on the tilapia work, sir."

"And is that what you and that IT nerd and another man were doing last night?"

"Oh that. Clive and I were just showing a friend how the machines work. He's a total dummy about anything scientific. I guess I was showing off a little. No harm done."

"I think not, Miss Worth. In fact, I know not. You never logged into our protocols but entered unauthorized samples. Your other friend was an unauthorized visitor. Miss Worth, AlphaGen is a team, a family. You have been moonlighting on projects unrelated to Golden Tilapia. That is not teamwork. That is not what I hired you for and pay you well for. You were headed to the top, Miss Worth, but you've proven you can't be trusted. As of this moment, you are terminated from AlphaGen, and you can forget about working in this field…anywhere."

The beeping of numbers being punched into a phone were audible through the intercom. "Okay, you two. It's time to move."

The door to the lab opened and two large goons burst in. Ashley was caught completely off guard but quickly recovered. She reached under the bench and unplugged her computer.

"Hello, gentlemen. What can I do for you?"

"Okay, lady. We can do this the easy way or the hard way. Your choice."

"Well, given your advantage in numbers, if not intellect, I suspect the easy way would be preferable."

"Roper said you'd prob'ly be a smartass. Let's go."

The two goons flanked Ashley, each grabbing an arm. Outraged, she shook them off, picked up her purse, and started walking out of the lab between them.

As they approached the door, and without turning around, she flipped the surveillance camera the bird. Then she paused.

"On second thought. Give me a moment, gentlemen. Okay?" She turned toward the camera. "Hey, Roper."

"What, Miss Worth?!"

Ashley turned back around and mooned the camera.

"Spunky dame," commented the first goon.

"Nice ass," said the other.

The two goons walked Ashley to her VW. The first goon took out his phone, punched in numbers, listened with the speaker on.

"Hello, Mr. R. We're at her car. What now?"

"Well, search it, idiot."

Goon number one walked around to the back of the VW and lifted the hood. He stared in, looking puzzled.

"My guess is you're unfamiliar with fine German engineering. The trunk's in the front."

Goon number one closed the hatch and walked around to the front, jerked on the handle. Nothing happened.

"Here, let me help," Ashley said.

She reached in through the driver's side, pulled the trunk latch. The first goon lifted the lid. The trunk was empty except for jumper cables, an old towel, and a box of tampons.

"Jesus, that stinks. There's nothin' in here, Mr. R. It smells like dead fish, but there ain't no fish or fish parts."

"Damn, she must have hidden them somewhere. Get the hell back here."

"Yes, sir. Happily. You're free to go, ma'am."

"Thank you, gentlemen. Have a nice day."

"After your behavior, our day's all downhill from here, ma'am."

Still holding on to her purse, Ashley got into her car and drove off.

CHAPTER 26

Late the next evening, Ashley dialed Clive. "Don't go to bed yet, Clive. I'm on my way there. Stuff's happening."

"Hold on, I'm coming."

Clive put down his soldering iron, flipped up the lid on his magnifying eyeglasses, turned off several pieces of electronic equipment, and went to the door.

"Hey, Ashley. I figured you'd try to get a good night's sleep before tomorrow's misadventures. What's up?"

"Lots." She told him about Flo, holding back tears. When she'd regained her composure, she recounted what happened at AlphaGen. "On top of all that, Roper canned me. He hijacked me in the lab. He must have video links at home and saw me working in the lab. He didn't have the courage to confront me face-to-face, so he sent a couple of henchmen, who threw me out of the building."

"Sounds like standard procedure for Roper. Did he tell you why?"

"He was more than a little unhinged, ranting and raving, but basically he said it was because I wasn't dedicated to the tilapia project. Little does he know. I tried to scramble the code on the Norwegian fish genes but got blocked."

"Oops," Clive interrupted.

"Oops?" Ashley asked. "What do you mean 'oops'?"

"I'm the reason you got blocked. When Roper hired me, he made me AlphaGen's CCS, meaning chief of cyber security. He was mainly worried about his system being hacked, being held for ransomware. He was all paranoid about threats to his little fiefdom from outside. I reminded him that the enemy might lie within, someone engaging in corporate espionage, hired by a competitor. He thought that was brilliant and spouted about the need for firewalls and guardrails. I finally convinced him to let me install a 'gotcha' program in the Golden Tilapia software, meaning, if someone messed with genetic codes that were working, they'd be kicked out of the system. And he'd be alerted."

"Well, it worked, Clive. Congratulations."

"Sorry."

"Anyway, after escorting me from the building, his boys tossed my car. I think they were looking for our shark fins. But it doesn't make sense. Why should Roper care about shark fins or shark genetics?"

"I think Roper's up to his eyeballs in alligators," Clive said. "Tilapia, sharks, Chang, who knows? As my momma would say, 'Trash will tell.' It seems like the puzzle pieces are falling into place. We just don't know what the puzzle is supposed to look like."

"I hope you're right. Maybe my getting canned by Roper was a sign that what we're doing tomorrow is really meaningful. In addition to saving the sharks, it would be great if it were some sort of retribution. We owe it to Flo."

Picking up a shopping bag at her feet, Ashley withdrew a bottle of low-budget champagne. "I stopped on my way here and picked this up. I want to celebrate my release from AlphaGen, and toast Flo's memory. And last, I want to gloat about our success wreaking mayhem on Roper and his cronies, in the event we're not around to celebrate tomorrow."

After dodging a ricocheting cork, they clinked glasses and drank a large portion of the bottle.

Ashley burped delicately and smiled. "You know, Clive. I'm in the mood to unburden. It's like what soldiers do before they go into battle, confess, clear their minds, make amends. But I feel I'm overdue for an accounting of my past and misspent youth, the parts I'm usually too embarrassed to reveal. It's the sort of thing I would have told Flo, but she's no longer with us. Do you mind?"

Clive, more than a little surprised and taken aback by her intimacy, said, "Sure, Ashley. If it will make you feel better. Confession is good for the soul."

"Great. Thank you. And stop me if you get bored."

"Unlikely."

"You probably don't know, Clive, I was married, once, shortly after I graduated from college with my journalism degree. I met my 'wasband' in a spin class at the gym. We'd been smiling politely at one another for several weeks, and I found him climbing on a bike closer to me each session. Eventually, we were on side-by-side exercycles, and I realized we were competing with one another during the sprint session that ended each class. One by one, the other riders fell out, and it was just me and the guy, going full bore, making the room shake. He finally gave up, red-faced and sweating, almost fell off his bike."

"Oh boy. Talk about performance anxiety."

"I guess so. I sprinted for another fifteen seconds to show I could – okay, to rub it in—and then coasted to a stop. The room, or at least the women in the room, applauded. Afterward, he met me at the juice bar, and we had a pleasant enough conversation, during which he begrudgingly congratulated me on my stamina. I thanked him for the compliment, kind of tossed it off as no big thing, that I enjoyed cycling. I kind of failed to mention that I had been captain of the Stanford cycling team as an undergraduate. A girl has to have her secrets, you know."

"And one thing led to another, I assume," Clive said.

"Oh yes. He invited me to dinner that night, picked me up in his Jaguar and took me to Benu, a three-star restaurant in the city. I learned he worked for an investment firm downtown, managed hedge funds, and didn't hide the fact that he made lots of money. I was painfully underpaid in my quest for a Pulitzer in Hollywood Gossip. The idea of finding a rich boyfriend had occurred to me from time to time."

"And one thing led to another?" Clive asked again, but with little enthusiasm.

"Are you wondering if I went to bed with him that night?"

"Uh, was I that obvious?"

"Yes. The answer is no. I had a personal dictum, a rule I lived by, that I would never go to bed with a man on the first date."

"That's probably wise," Clive said. "How long was it before your next date?"

"Um. Well, if I remember correctly, it was the next evening."

Clive didn't say anything.

Ashley went on. "So, we started seeing each other more and more, mostly on weekends. By day, we'd do marathons in the Berkeley Hills, and at night we'd do marathons in his house on Russian Hill, overlooking the Bay. We went white-water kayaking, helicopter snowboarding, rock climbing, sky diving, scuba diving, caving, and he paid for it all, provided all my equipment. We joined an underwater spelunking club and started cave diving, really technical stuff. On a dry caving trip in New Mexico, he totally surprised me. We were worming our way for the better part of an hour, just the two of us, mostly on our bellies, through passages so tight we had to take our packs off and push them through ahead."

"Gack! As a certified claustrophobic, I'm trying hard not to imagine what you're describing," Clive said.

"Cramped would be an exaggeration. But it was another thing we sort of competed at, like who could tolerate the most discomfort. So, the last passage opened up into a beautiful room where we could finally stand up. He had apparently gone ahead the day before and placed candles on this little shelf, like an altar, their light flickering and reflecting and glowing off the stalagmites and stalactites. He took a bottle of champagne and two glasses from his pack—how they hadn't broken was a miracle—and proposed a toast, to us. Then he produced a diamond ring. You can't imagine how it seemed to explode in the candlelight. And he proposed. I was blown away. What could I say but yes? I did, all choked up with tears."

"Yeah, I can see where that would have been very romantic," Clive offered quietly.

"You have no idea. The mood wasn't even spoiled when he pulled out a two-page, stapled document from his backpack and said, 'By the way, I had a prenuptial agreement drawn up. Let's sign it right here.' Which I did, without reading it. Between the dim light and my tears, I couldn't have read it if I tried. We honeymooned in Aruba, but things plunged downhill pretty fast. I guess marriage must have made him feel like a caged animal. He turned out to be a total control freak, of everything we did and everything I did. He treated me like a helpless Disney princess. We fought more and made love less."

"At least you had the Jaguar," Clive offered.

"No way! I wasn't allowed to drive it. He claimed it was too technical. I finally started getting nervous about his behavior and began paying more attention. At one point, I suspected he was going through my things, like medications…like birth control pills, in particular. So, I put the tiniest strip of clear tape across the latching mechanism and sure enough, he had opened it. I was relieved to find nothing amiss. I mean the last thing I wanted at the time was to have kids. I guess he wanted to make sure I was taking them. About that time, I decided I should read the prenuptial agreement I had signed without reading, what began my journey into uninformed consent. I finally found it hidden in his stack of men's magazines, tucked in among the pages of a brutally graphic disquisition on erectile dysfunction."

"Do I detect a seismic moment?" Clive asked.

"That's putting it mildly. I had no idea what I'd gotten myself in for. The prenup must have been drawn up by an attorney at Shyster and Sons. I had agreed not to gain more than twenty-five pounds at any time. If I got pregnant, which was to be avoided 'by all means possible'—of course, entirely on my part—any weight gain would have to be lost within six months after a child was born. There was some drop-dead terminology about extramarital affairs. It went on, but the final paragraph is pretty much burned in my mind, given that I reread it, like, twenty times. It said the conditions put forth in this agreement supersede all state and federal laws regarding joint ownership of property and in the eventuality of termination of this contractual arrangement—I mean we didn't have a marriage, we had a contractual arrangement—all property would revert to the original owner or purchaser. The only thing I owned was my VW."

"Damn good cars, despite being designed by Hitler," Clive offered.

"Uh, right. Anyway, I began digging. I didn't have to dig too deeply. I figured I'd start with the tender moment when he proposed in the candlelit cavern. I contacted some of the folks in the spelunking club that we no longer belonged to. They were only too eager to talk, because my hubby was universally disliked. They had tolerated him through two previous marriages, another revelation. Both involved women who were strikingly similar in body shape and size to me, which explained all the perfectly fitting sports gear he 'acquired' for me. And it turns out he had hired a couple of the other cavers to go put the candles in that room. The asshole had weaponized romance. And then the dickhead argued afterward about how much they had agreed to be paid."

"Sounds like a stellar individual," Clive offered, a little more enthusiastically than before.

"Pick your favorite characterization," Ashley said. "I think of him as the spawn of Satan. Basically, he was a total narcissist, a great self-promoter, and a total failure as a human being. Anyway, it all ended at his company's annual Christmas party. I got into a heated argument with one of his coworkers about the ethics of their business practices and needed some space. While looking for a bathroom, I found myself in the master bedroom, and there he was, with two bimbo secretaries from the office whom he had charmed into bed."

"Rule number one," Clive said. "Don't dip into the secretarial pool."

"He didn't follow many rules, except the ones he made, which he readily broke. I took an Uber home, loaded up my VW, and left without a note. The divorce papers found me at work about a week later."

Clive remained silent, obviously processing all this. Ashley broke the awkwardness.

"I swore to give up men, then and there. And I did, for a while. Started hanging out with my girlfriends. Lots of fun, no complications. I had really enjoyed scuba diving, so I saved up and bought my own equipment. I met Luke on a dive trip."

"From what I've seen of Luke, he seems very unlike your ex."

"Exactly. One hundred eighty degrees different. Laid back, carefree, unambitious, dazed and confused, goofy. Guileless, without pretense. Not that he'd know what that means. For me, his cluelessness was a breath of fresh air. The only thing the two of them had in common, my weakness I guess, was his hunkiness."

Clive moved uncomfortably in his seat.

"But you can only spend so much time between the sheets," she added.

"That's what I always say," Clive offered, weakly.

"Luke and I have stayed friends. And I'm off men again."

Clive remained quiet.

Ashley filled the silence. "So, those are the sordid details of my failed relationships. But enough about me, TMI. You never talk about your social life, Clive. Like, if you have a girlfriend. I'd think with your brains and earning power, they'd be standing in line outside your door."

"I wish that were true," Clive said. "But regrettably, it's not. End of story."

"Clive! Did you just use the subjunctive?"

"What? Oh yeah, I guess so. Kind of automatic."

"Automatic?" Ashley said. "Maybe for point-one-percent of the population, meaning former English majors like me, not computer nerds like you."

"Hey," Clive reacted, his voice defensive. "Inner city schools aren't as bad as they're cracked up to be. I had a very demanding English teacher in high school, before I dropped out. She insisted that good grammar was a ticket out of the ghetto."

"If you ask me," Ashley replied. "It's more like a ticket to low-paying jobs, and a lot less lucrative than computer programming. I think you made the right career decision."

"Yeah. I guess so. Ironic, too, given that most of the people I've worked with in IT, male or female, were foreign nationals on H-1B visas and weren't impressed with my grammar, given they hardly spoke English."

Ashley smiled. "At least they had an excuse. And now I've strayed from my real reason for coming here, which wasn't to bore you with my memoir. There's something else, more immediate, on my mind."

"What's that?" Clive asked quickly, happy to change the subject.

"I'm beginning to agree with you about how much disbelief we should be willing to suspend."

"How's that?"

"Something doesn't add up."

"Are we going to revisit my arithmetic failings again?"

"No, not that. What I mean is the attack on the Asian divers. It was just too easy to say they were attacked because they were Asian, like some of the fishermen on the *Stinky Wrinkle*. I mean there were Anglos on the boat, and Hispanics too. We're missing something. We need to know more about those divers. I can't help but think something about their behavior triggered that attack. Any ideas?"

"Well, for starters," Clive said after a moment's reflection. "It seems like a dozen people dying, regardless of ethnicities, should have drawn some attention. Like a news report somewhere in the local media. But that hasn't happened."

"Unless the local media was discouraged from publicizing the attack. Bad for business, scare tourists away."

"Historical precedent, you know," Clive said. "Maybe we should petition to have the town renamed Amity."

"With all the death and dismemberment, Amityville might be more appropriate," Ashley replied. "But maybe we should look at media sources that would be less concerned with local tourism and more concerned with the welfare of Asians. Can we do that?"

"Easy," Clive answered. "I'll scan Chinese media outlets."

His fingers again flew across his keyboard as Ashley watched. "Here we go. Weibo, WeChat, Baidu. Now to sift through local postings from our area on these sites," Clive mumbled to himself. "Okay. Found one. Now search for missing Asian visitors in our region… Bingo. Listen to this: 'Concern has grown over the disappearance of a party of scuba divers from the Guangdong region of China. Six couples, honeymooning together, left for a morning dive on board the dive boat *Calypso V*, which returned to port minus all twelve. Local authorities have been uncooperative in investigating their disappearance, suggesting they may have defected and are in hiding. Friends and relatives are understandably concerned, as is Bingwen Bao, the manager of FusionAsia Restaurant. Bingwen claims the couples ordered an elaborate dinner the evening before the dive trip and insisted on paying in renminbi instead of dollars, which the manager can't convert. The local consulate is actively pursuing this disappearance while relatives await news of their missing loved ones.'"

"Wait," Ashley said. "Isn't that the same restaurant where we saw the picketers who were protesting shark fin soup on the menu?"

"Whoa! You're right. Are you thinking what I'm thinking?"

"What are you thinking?" Ashley asked.

"That the restaurant manager has a fat chance of getting his money, given we know those diners became dinner for a bunch of sharks."

"That too," Ashley said. "But, more importantly, maybe, just maybe, they had shark fin soup that night and somehow the sharks sensed it. But that's idle speculation. I think we need to pay Mr. Bingwen Bao a visit."

"Is this a date?" Clive asked, less than enthusiastically.

Ashley smiled. "Why not?"

Clive jumped up and grabbed his keys. "When you put it that way, I'll drive. And I'll even open the passenger door for you."

CHAPTER 27

"Nice car," Ashley said as they drove off. "Isn't this a Tesla?"

"It's the X model, pretty much top of the line, unless you want to go for the muscle version."

"Was pink and white an option?" Ashley asked.

"I didn't consult with my sister," Clive answered.

"Without being too snoopy," Ashley said, obviously being snoopy. "I'm finding it hard to believe Roper is paying you enough to afford something like this."

"Right. On my salary, even with the perks, I'd be driving a newer model of your Beetle. But I managed to sock away the earnings from my brief venture into robotic toys."

"You mean when the government shut you down, they didn't clean out your bank account?"

"Oh, they got that, alright," Clive said. "But I'd squirreled away most of the profits in cryptocurrency, which was untraceable and untouchable."

"Smart move, I guess," Ashley said. "For ill-gotten gains." But she smiled as she said the last part.

Traffic was a bitch, parking downtown even worse. Strangely, several parking places were open right in front of the restaurant, under the trees. Clive started to back his dark blue Tesla into one when he noticed that nearby cars were covered in white blotches. As a large splotch of crow excrement plopped on his windshield, he thought better of it.

They finally found a safe spot three blocks from restaurant row, just as it started to rain. Clive pulled a unicorn-themed umbrella from under the driver's seat. "A present from my sister. Should work for rain, or crow poop."

Two protestors, both cold, wet, and miserable, were picketing out front of FusionAsia, their pithy painted statements barely legible, running down soggy cardboard. The protestors hardly reacted when Clive and Ashley passed by.

"Oh good," Ashley said. "The menu is posted outside." She walked up to the case, wiped raindrops off the glass, and stared. "Damn, it's in Chinese."

"Yeah, right, hold on," Clive said, moving alongside her. "Here it is, Soups." He ran his finger down the menu list, stopped two-thirds of the way down. "Right, it says 'Soup of fin'—or that could be the character for wing—of shark. Whoa! Sixty dollars a bowl. Maybe we should get a pizza instead."

"Clive! You can read Chinese?"

"Not as well as Russian. Both were indispensable during my hacking and game development days. Those guys are light years ahead of us in robotics."

"Clive, you never fail to amaze me," Ashley exclaimed.

Inside, the restaurant was dimly lit, with traditional Asian decor and a small fountain with large goldfish swimming in a pool, next to the cash register. The air smelled of sesame oil and ginger. A woman in a long black silk dress embroidered with red dragons approached them.

"Good evening. Do you have a reservation?" she said in slightly accented English.

"Uh, no," Ashley answered. "We hoped we could drop in for a light meal."

"Well, normally a reservation would be required. But the weather must be keeping people away. I think I can find seating for a couple. Would you like to see the menu?" She handed Clive one, before Ashley could answer.

They looked at the menu, which was in English. Clive ran his finger down to the soups. "Hmm. Nothing about shark fin. It was right between the Gu qiao mi xian and the yangrou paomo. Do you think our protestors have had an impact?"

"More likely, Anglo customers seldom ask for it. Why invite trouble?"

Clive agreed. "Hmm, this is interesting. At the bottom, it says that FusionAsia is part of Chang Enterprises. Wasn't the guy Roper talked to during that instant messaging session named Chang?"

"Yes. You're right. But that's a pretty common Chinese name. Let's file it away, just in case."

Staying in their budget, they ordered wonton soup and a bowl of noodles each. When the waitress/hostess brought the check, Clive, in excellent Cantonese, said, "That was superb. Would it be inappropriate to pay a compliment to the manager?"

The hostess smiled, and answered in English. "Of course not. That would be appreciated. Give me a moment, please, and I'll get Mr. Bingwen."

Ashley grinned at Clive.

Bingwen Bao was short by any measure. He wore a dark brown suit, a darker tie, and too much cologne. He looked more than a little harried but approached their table and bowed slightly. "Yes?" he said in English. "Our hostess said you would like to talk with me. How can I help you?"

Clive greeted him in Chinese, obviously more than a simple hello. Bingwen stood up straight and smiled. "Your

Chinese is quite good," he said in English. "The chef will appreciate the compliment. But how is it that you can help me?"

"In addition to having had a wonderful meal," Clive laid it on, "we need information. We are, in truth, private investigators, hired by families of six Chinese couples who disappeared recently. The trail has gone cold, except that we have learned that they all dined here the night before they vanished. We're hoping you can tell us something, anything, about their behavior that night. What they wore, what they ate, whether they drank too much, did they leave credit card information? Anything would be helpful at this point."

Bingwen grew agitated. He burst out in Chinese, a long rant. Clive put up his hand. "That's all helpful," Clive said. "But I'd appreciate if you'd repeat that in English, for the benefit of my partner here, who will be taking notes. I got the part about them stiffing you."

"So sorry, miss," Bingwen said as he turned to Ashley. "They had the most expensive dishes on the menu, several rounds of dim sum, bird's nest and shark fin soup, stewed sea cucumber, braised abalone. And they paid me in Chinese currency. My boss has given strict orders to only accept US dollars or international credit cards. But it's been really hard lately to find help, and we had a new cashier who apparently hadn't paid attention. I'm responsible for the loss, and apologizing hourly to an angry overlord."

"Your boss sounds rather unreasonable," Ashley said.

"If you only knew," Bingwen replied. "Unfortunately, I have nothing further to add. But I would appreciate if you let me know what you find. You could get me out of hot water."

"Most certainly," Clive said. "I'll have to ask the families first, but after your helpfulness, I can't see them saying no. And, truly, our meal was delicious and—"

Bingwen's phone buzzed. He looked at it. "Damn, here we go again." He hurried off, listening and speaking to his phone.

Clive and Ashley paid their bill, in cash, picked up the unicorn umbrella, and walked outside to clearing skies and a clean, fresh outdoors smell, except for the crow guano. They high-fived each other.

Ashley was all smiles. "Idle speculation confirmed. I'm thinking our divers reeked of shark fin soup and that caused the attack."

"Good thing there weren't any enraged sea cucumbers or abalone around also."

"You're not throwing me off the scent, forgive the pun. I'm convinced my incredibly stupid, dangerous plan is a good idea."

"I wouldn't go so far as to say it's a good idea any more than before, but at least it's a little more justified."

"I'll live with that."

It was getting toward midnight when they got back to Clive's apartment. Clive yawned and said, "Dawn is going to come early tomorrow. We should probably call it a night."

"I agree, Clive. But I never finished my memoir. Or at least I didn't bring it up to date."

"I thought you'd sworn off men again," Clive said. "I guess you've found a new and acceptable hunk."

"Yes, and no," Ashley replied. "Or no, and yes. I've finally come to realize that hunkiness is cheap, vastly overrated, more an attractive nuisance than anything. And I now know that I need mental and emotional stimulation a lot more. I've turned over a new leaf, changed my ways, come to my senses, or some such platitude. I haven't been on a bike in over two years and I don't even own a pair of running shoes. I've decided, after experiencing my ex and Luke and what they brought to my life, that my values were misplaced. And I think I've discovered where they should be."

She leaned over and kissed Clive lightly on the lips.

"You know, Clive. Given all the time we've spent together, and the things we've done, I don't think tonight was our first date."

CHAPTER 28

Early the next morning, Clive awoke, rolled over and saw Ashley sleeping peacefully beside him. He blinked, twice, then pinched himself. Twice.

Moving slowly, he slipped out of bed and headed for the kitchen, hoping to make coffee that she might find tolerable. He passed over his usual jar of instant and found, deep in the freezer, something more authentic. While brewing the coffee, he mentally thanked all those hunks on whom Ashley had honed her skills.

The aroma of coffee must have wafted into the bedroom. Clive looked up to see Ashley standing in the doorway, smiling and wearing only a t-shirt, one of his that said, "The geeks shall inherit the earth." She sat down and he poured a cup, which she drank, without grimacing.

"Clive, I hate to kiss and run, but I've got to go recover our shark fins before we reconnoiter with Luke at *Calypso*."

"And I have to finish assembling the electronic stuff that you so rudely interrupted last night."

Ashley leaned over and gave Clive a very sloppy kiss, slipped on her clothes ("I've got to cover up all these bite marks"), and left. Clive pinched himself, twice, then returned to his workbench.

An hour later, Ashley pushed a cart carrying a small cooler and three cardboard boxes containing the fins down a ramp to the *Calypso*. Black smoke pulsed out of the exhaust pipe on top of the pilot house, filling the morning air with the stench of diesel. Ashley handed the boxes across to Luke but kept hold of the cooler. When Luke set the boxes down on a corner of the deck, they pulsated even more distinctly.

"Hmmm," Ashley muttered. "That's weird. It's like those boxes are shaking. But so is this old boat. My imagination is working in overdrive. Must be nerves."

While Luke was assembling dive gear on the stern, he glanced down the dock at a nearby canoe. "Whoa. Now there's some sloppy seamanship. Somebody tied that baby up with like a piece of string. It's gonna float off and be a hazard to navigation."

He started to walk down the dock when Ashley shouted at him, "Luke! Come on, for Christ's sake. Don't go playing Boy Scout now. We've got too much stuff to do before we can leave."

Luke ignored her and started to tie the canoe up. "Hey! There's like blood all over this thing. And there's a dead shark and like a boot, or half a boot, and...JEEZUS! Come look at this!"

Ashley, annoyed and impatient, hurried off the *Calypso* and joined Luke on the dock.

"This better be goo—Oh my god."

She reached down and gingerly picked up a partial red cowboy boot. It contained a foot and a few inches of ankle. That's when she noticed a dead baby shark on the floor.

"Didn't the mayor, the guy who got attacked during the boat parade, always wear red cowboy boots?" she asked.

"Yeah, I think so. But I doubt he wore shorties."

"No, this isn't a short boot. It's been bitten off. Look at the jagged edge. And that baby shark isn't big enough to have done that. He, or rather she, could only have swallowed it after somebody else chopped it into pieces. You know what this means, don't you?"

"Sharks dig leather and someone's using boots for bait?"

"No, dammit. It means our sharks are reproducing, and they're smart enough to chop up food to feed their young. Which means we have a bigger and growing problem if we don't pull things off today."

Their attention was drawn to Clive, who was coming down the dock, struggling with several fiberglass suitcases.

"Good," she said. "Let's get going. We'll fill Clive in on all this later. We can call the police on our way out, tell them enough to get their interest. They can figure out the rest for themselves."

Clive climbed aboard the *Calypso* and unpacked a medium-sized, black case that contained a small video monitor and a small speaker. Ashley and Clive, smiling at one another, tossed lines onto the dock and pulled up fenders while Luke slowly moved *Calypso* out into the harbor.

"I never got to tell you how sorry I am about Flo," Clive said as they approached the last navigation marker in the harbor channel. "You guys were close. It would be hard to work at AlphaGen without her, or you."

Ashley stifled a sniffle, squared her shoulders. "She was a good person, much more than just a work colleague. I'm going to miss her. I'm determined to somehow make things right, even though I'm not at AlphaGen anymore."

"Agreed. And it looks like we're in the same boat, pardon the pun."

"How's that?" Ashley asked.

"I got toasted too. Roper texted me this morning, after you left, didn't give a reason, only said I'd be hearing from my parole officer first thing."

"Ouch. I think it's because he saw you in the lab with Luke and me when we were analyzing those shark fins. It seems like everything I touch turns to shit. I'm sorry I dragged you into this."

"Hey, no biggie, no need to apologize. It's not the first time for me. Fortunately, my skills seem to be in demand."

"So, you're not mad?"

"Hell no," Clive answered emphatically. "It would be an understatement to say that I like the way things have worked out. I mean, I should *thank* Roper for bringing us together. And this shark fin escapade is way more interesting than being a corporate IT call girl."

"So, you're still game to go?"

"Fer sure."

"I don't know how to thank you enough, Clive." Ashley threw her arms around him and planted another wet one. Clive glanced nervously up at the wheelhouse, then returned the kiss. He broke it off and said, "Um, shouldn't we look at the stuff I put together?"

"Sure," Ashley said, smiling. "Let's see it."

Calypso came to a sudden halt.

"Hey, Luke. What's happening?" Ashley shouted. "Why are we stopping? We need to get moving, pronto."

"A little incoming traffic, Ashley. Not enough room in the channel for everybody."

Ashley and Clive looked ahead. Luke's comment was, if anything, an understatement. Filling the entire channel and headed at them, towering over *Calypso*, was a huge boat, a megayacht. Gleaming white with dark windows, multiple electronic domes on top. Scurrying around were several crewmembers carrying ropes and fenders, all clad in identical khaki pants and blue windbreakers with gold lettering. As the yacht passed them and left *Calypso* rocking in its wake, the stern became visible. A helicopter sat perched on the expansive rear deck. Written on the side of the chopper and in foot-high letters across the stern of the boat was the yacht's name: *Excalibur*.

"*White Privilege* would be more appropriate," Clive commented.

Calypso resumed her course, unimpressed.

Clive went back to opening the black case and showing Ashley the fruits of his labor. He removed a six-inch-long, cigar-shaped transmitter with a trailing wire. Putting on rubber gloves, he rummaged through Ashley's boxes until he found the biggest dorsal fin.

"These things don't smell any better than on the day we stole them. Whew."

Using a drill and cable ties, Clive attached the transmitter to the fin. The fin squirmed a little in the process.

"Hmm, these things must still have sensitive nerve endings or something. That's a little creepy."

Clive slid a tiny black switch on the transmitter. The small speaker started emitting beeps; a blinking light appeared on a map on the monitor.

"Good. It knows where we are. Hurdle number one."

"Please bring me up to speed, Clive. I'm dying to know what you're doing."

"Oh, sorry. I forget what is and isn't obvious. This little baby is a combo acoustic and radio transmitter. It sends out both ultrasonic and radio frequency information. The ultrasound signals are picked up underwater when we hang this transponding omni-directional hydrophone overboard."

He held up an object that looked like a cross between a holy water dispenser and a dildo, but with a cord attached.

"Whenever a shark comes to the surface and exposes its dorsal fin, a signal is sent up to a satellite that is relayed to my base station here. That way, we get exact location, date, local time, depth, speed, emotional state…just kidding on the last part. The beeps you're hearing are the signal that's being picked up. All the information is stored on a hard drive for later retrieval."

"Wow!" Ashley said. "You designed and built all this stuff yourself?"

"Well, sort of. The design is based on transmitters developed by a company in Nova Scotia, a site I visit frequently when I'm messing with robotics. I found the plans for one of their latest transmitters and quickly reverse engineered it, a technique I learned from my Russian hacker buddies. Same with the receiver and software. I tweaked the design a little, added redundancy to the system. Mainly, the ultrasonic tag transfers its data to the radio tag, so we get all the information at once. If it's as good as the company claims, the battery should last at least a month. This gizmo should have an over-the-horizon range of more than twenty-five miles, depending on satellite availability. Blame Canada if it doesn't work."

"I repeat. Wow! And I had a funny thought."

"A little levity right now might be good," Clive said.

"Well, not funny, like ha ha. It's more like irony. You remember the nutty professor at the town meeting? And his cockamamie ideas about shark fins broadcasting signals into space? You're making his dreams come true. And we're the mother ship."

Clive turned to Ashley. "I'm glad you're able to see a light side to all this. I'm less sanguine. My part is easy, no risk involved, except for a little patent infringement. Okay, a lot of patent infringement. That's all minor. Your part is different, way riskier. Are you sure you want to do this? Seems kind of crazy. In fact, it's downright foolhardy. Did you ever consider doing this out of one of those shark cages?"

"Not for very long," Ashley answered. "First, it would be hard to find one, especially a good one, on such short notice. Second, I'm afraid all the metal in the cage might interfere with the electromagnetics, if that's how the sharks orient to their fins and vice versa. And third, it's an unproven technology, too many moving parts, prone to failure, even at only 4.7 meters down."

"I guess so. Still, those sharks are killers. What if you're wrong?"

"Then I guess you'll just have to drive the boat back alone," she said.

A black SUV with darkened windows came speeding down the dock and screeched to a halt. The two goons from the previous night leapt out, packing heat, and ran down a gangway to a sleek red powerboat with three huge, idling outboards on the stern. They were barely aboard when the powerboat sped off, throwing a large wave over a white buoy that said "Reduce Speed, No Wake."

Calypso slowed as it reached the Cousteau Reserve buoy, which Clive managed to snag with a boat hook on the third try. Luke already had two sets of dive gear laid out on the stern.

"Time to suit up, fearless leader," he said to Ashley.

"I'm not so sure about being fearless," Ashley replied. "I can feel butterflies fluttering around in my stomach, or something like that." She stopped. "Wow. I almost forgot the most important part." She motioned for Clive to join them.

Opening the cooler she'd brought on board, Ashley produced a small, tightly sealed plastic jar with a brown, screw-on lid. A milky white, viscous liquid sloshed around inside.

"Cool," Luke said. "We're having a pre-dive gelato snack. Is that the Caribbean coconut flavor?"

"Hardly," Ashley answered. "This is the mission critical component that's going to join the shark fins with their rightful owners. It's synthetic barnacle glue."

"Say what?" Luke asked.

"Barnacle glue. The strongest, most waterproof, fastest setting, nontoxic adhesive in the world."

"And where in the world does one obtain a jar full of synthetic barnacle glue?" It was Clive's turn. "Ebay? Etsy? Amazon?"

"No, it's more a black-market product, or at least I'm not really authorized to have it."

"No surprise there," Clive said. "I'd be surprised if you let something like that deter you. So, fess up, time's a wasting."

"Right. So, one of the guys in the cave explorers' group I told you about last night is a marine chemist. I called him a couple of days ago and explained my incomplete plan to return the fins to the sharks. He was fascinated, although skeptical."

"Not the first," Clive offered.

"Skeptical but intrigued. I explained that completion of my hare-brained plan involved several not-completely-thought-through steps, chief among which was making the fins stick back on the sharks. I'd remembered him talking about this top secret, Navy-funded research grant, where he got to work on marine-fouling organisms, all the things that stick to ship bottoms and slow them down. He immediately saw the relevance and explained about the wonderful properties of barnacle cement, the stuff a baby barnacle uses to glue itself to a rock, whale, or nuclear submarine. His research got him to the point where he could synthesize the stuff in small quantities, like a pint at a time, but they hadn't come up with an antidote…something to coat ship bottoms to keep barnacle-produced glue from working and thus keep barnacles from attaching. So, they had lots of the glue lying around, and he admitted it would be interesting to know if it would work gluing fins to sharks. He overnighted it to me."

"In a gelato jar?" Clive asked.

"That made it easier to smuggle it out of his lab and not raise suspicions. He hid it in a well-insulated lunch box. It has to stay cool until it's spread on the surface of the thing you want to attach. That's what the little basting brushes are for. We have to baste the fins with the glue. We have like thirty minutes before it becomes inactive."

Ashley handed out rubber gloves. "Don't get any on your fingers or they'll stick together forever," she warned.

The three quickly spread the milky substance on the cut surfaces of the shark fins, then carefully returned the fins to their boxes, making sure the glue-covered parts weren't touching anything.

"Like I said before," Luke repeated. "Time to suit up, fearless leader."

He and Ashley hopped around, struggling into their wetsuits. As he was about to pull his neoprene pants up,

Ashley looked at his left leg, where a small Minnie Mouse Band-Aid was affixed to the calf.

"Isn't that where the shark bit you? It doesn't look that bad."

"Oh that. Yeah, kind of a false alarm. Just a flesh wound, I guess. Like I said, the guy bit me where I had my trusty dive knife strapped to my leg. I bet he has a toothache."

"She, Luke. Remember, we're dealing with lady sharks. Don't go regendering them."

Ashley attempted to spit in her mask to keep it from fogging. Nothing happened. "Wow. I've got no spit. I guess I'm more than a little scared after all."

Trusty dive knife in place, Luke picked up two of the boxes of shark fins and tucked one under each arm. Ashley picked up the other box.

"Ready?" he said. Ashley gave him a thumbs up. "Good. One last thing. Please, please, please. Don't pee in your wetsuit. It like sends the sharks into a feeding frenzy."

"Very funny, Luke. No wonder the girls find you irresistible."

She stepped to the edge of the dive platform on the stern, spoke through the mike in her mask. "Hey, Clive, honey. Can you hear me with all this crap on?"

"Loud, if not clear. Good luck. Break a leg."

"I'm just hoping we bring them all back. Okay. This is for Flo."

The two divers dropped into the water and descended. They landed on the bottom amidst scuba tanks and weight belts atop shredded, color-coordinated wetsuits.

"I guess this is the right place," Ashley said. "More than a little creepy."

Clive lowered the hydrophone into the water and watched the monitor in the case he had brought. A blinking light appeared on the screen map and beeps emitted from the speaker. Data began scrolling across the monitor's screen.

"I've got a strong signal up here," he said. "Everything okay down there?"

"Hunky dory," Ashley replied. "Nobody down here but us…whoa. Look at that."

Sharks appeared out of the gloom, moving in formation, led by the one with legs and a tail fin. They began squirming and circling, followed closely by their freely swimming young.

"Oh boy," Luke said. "Here we go again. Hello boys, I'm ba-ack."

"For Pete's sake, Luke. They're girls, remember. And it looks like I guessed right about them having babies."

Ashley did a three-sixty, assessing the situation. "Okay, grab a box but don't open it until I say so. I think they have to be real close."

"I don't think you have to worry about them not getting close."

As if on cue, the sharks moved toward the divers and began circling.

Clive could hear everything Luke and Ashley were saying through the speaker in *Calypso*'s wheelhouse, even while standing near the side of the boat and staring intently at their bubbles. His concentration was shattered by a high-pitched sound in the distance.

Gazing over the stern, looking toward the shore, he saw a red powerboat speeding toward them, a huge rooster tail shooting out from behind. A man was standing up and waving something.

"Not a very smart thing to be doing in a fast-moving boat," Clive said.

The speedboat came to an abrupt halt right next to the *Calypso*, its substantial wake rocking the dive boat. The arm waver was goon number one, and what he was waving was an automatic rifle that he now pointed at Clive.

"Uh-oh. Looks like things are about to get interesting," Clive mumbled.

The goon shouted over the noise of the outboards, "Where is she?"

"Who would that be?" Clive asked, trying to hide his discomfort at having a gun pointed at him.

"The dame from the lab."

"Dame?" Clive asked. "You're going to have to be more specific. You mean like Judi Dench, or Elizabeth Nneka Anionwu?"

"Don't be a wise-ass. The dame with our fins."

"Oh. That would be Ashley. She's down there," Clive said, pointing to the bubbles coming up between the two boats.

"Get her up here fast, with the fins." He pointed the gun upward and fired off a loud burst.

"Okay, but you don't have to get pushy."

Clive grabbed the microphone. "Hey, guys, we got company up here, and it's not the cavalry."

After a pause, Ashley spoke, her voice garbled from excited breathing. "Clive, now's not the time to be cute. We've got some very unhappy looking sharks all around us, and I hope they just want their fins back. What's happening up there?"

"I guess you could say the same up here," Clive answered. "Except the predators here are three unhappy guys in a speedboat with guns, and I *know* they want their fins back."

"Oh shit. OH SHIT!" Ashley shouted as she twisted around to see one of the sharks behind her break from the circle and head straight for her, its mouth wide open.

It was about to attack, when the shark with the tail fin and legs shot between Ashley's legs and rammed the attacking shark.

"Damn!" was all Ashley could mutter.

The sharks regrouped and began circling again, the circle tightening. All the sharks turned toward the divers in a deliberate, coordinated attack.

"NOW!" Ashley shouted.

Turning two boxes upside down, Ashley and Luke started dumping fins out. Instead of falling to the sea floor, the fins propelled themselves out of the boxes.

The sharks stopped instantly and began nosing the fins. The fins, in response, moved independently toward the sharks. As if pulled by strings, the fins lined up on the backs, sides, and tails of the sharks and attached themselves.

"Holy shit!" Ashley shouted. "It's actually working!" Her voice revealed her pride.

"Holy shit!" Luke shouted, even louder. His voice revealed amazement.

Ashley regained her composure and opened the third box. The remaining fins practically leapt out and attached to sharks.

With fins intact, the sharks began rolling around in ecstasy, swimming loops and doing barrel rolls. All but one shark had been reunited with its fins, the exception being one still missing a tail fin.

The sharks circled Ashley and Luke one more time and then began to leave, except for the shark that had Clive's transmitter attached to its dorsal fin. It swam at Luke and bit at his leg.

"Hey! NO!"

But the shark only grabbed his dive knife in her mouth, pulled it out of its holster, and joined its mates. Then all the sharks swam off in formation, except two sharks that lined up on either side of the tailless shark, which they helped keep up with the group.

Luke looked down at his now-empty dive knife holster. "I guess your luck ran out, old buddy."

The victorious twosome slowly ascended amidst their bubbles, surfacing between the *Calypso* and the speedboat, facing Clive.

Luke lifted his mask off his face and shouted to Ashley, "It worked! You're a frigging genius."

Ashley waved to Clive happily. He put his finger to his lips, hushing her and pointed to the speedboat. The goon in the boat let go with a burst from his automatic rifle. Ashley and Luke spun around, facing the intruders. "Uh-oh, I see what you mean."

"Okay, lady, give us the fins."

"Uh, s-sorry guys. Looks like you're a day late to the party. You'll have to get them back from our friends down there. And I don't think they're feeling especially generous."

"Hey, boss," the second goon said. "This sucks. Whaddr we gonna do with them?"

Goon number one pointed his rifle down at Ashley and Luke. Ashley screamed. The goon aimed between them and let go with a long, loud burst, clearly out of frustration. The surface exploded from the bullets.

"Get outta the water," he commanded.

A bit shaken, the two divers managed to pull themselves up on the boat's stern platform. Everyone stood still, dripping, waiting.

"I guess we'll take them back to Roper and let him decide."

Ashley turned and whispered to Clive, "These are my friends from the lab, the guys who tossed my car. Roper really wants those fins. Chang must have him by the short hairs!"

The goons commanded everyone out of their dive gear and into the speedboat, reinforced with a waving automatic rifle.

But as the three were about to climb in, the air shook with a distinctive thump-thump-thump. Looking up, they saw an approaching armada of helicopter gunships descending in their direction.

"Awright!" Clive exclaimed. "This time it *does* look like the cavalry."

"Shit!" the head goon yelled. "Forget these jerks. Let's get the hell out of here! Fast."

As directed, the driver of the power boat floored it, throwing the other two goons awkwardly to the floorboards. The goon with the rifle landed hard, his finger still on the trigger, causing the automatic weapon to fire off several rounds. Fortunately, the bullets went skyward as the boat sped off under the approaching helicopters.

The *Calypso*'s crew watched the speedboat disappear toward shore, while the helicopters drew closer.

"Quick," she said. "Let's check that tracking device."

All three huddled in front of the monitor and watched as the shark's signal moved quickly across the screen, toward its edge.

"I guess they got what they wanted, and now they're leaving," Clive said. "You were right all along. Two problems solved. Bigger problem headed our way."

In the helicopters, the copilot of the lead craft consulted the screen in front of him. "I see the target area directly ahead, sir. We're oh-one minute from the drop point. But it looks like a civilian craft is in the drop zone."

The pilot, Red Leader, didn't hesitate. "Truth, the environment, and collateral damage are the first casualties of war. We have our orders."

He lowered his visor, adjusted his bomb sights, looked left and right at his wing men.

"All wings report," Red Leader announced, his transmission audible through Calypso's radio.

The left wing helicopter pilot checked in. "Red Two standing by."

"Red Three standing by."

"Red Four, or am I Five, standing by. I can't remember. Whatever was in that hookah last night was paralyzing. I am so fucked up."

"Break. Break. This is Tower Sector 7. Transmitting aircraft, please identify yourself."

"No way, man. I'm not that fucked up."

In *Calypso*'s wheelhouse, the gallant threesome watched as the helicopters grew closer and lower.

Ashley grabbed the radio mike. "Attack helicopters! Attack helicopters! This is the *Calypso*."

There was nothing but static.

Ashley turned to Luke in desperation. "Wasn't this thing working a moment ago?"

Luke fumbled with the device, but again all they heard was static. "It's a little temperamental."

He bashed the mike hard against the steering wheel. They heard voices over the speaker. "Okay, try it now."

Ashley keyed the mike. "Attack helicopters. This is the *Calypso*. We have, uh, neutralized all the sharks. They have left the area. Please do not attack. I repeat. The sharks are neutralized. Please abort your attack."

"Are you sure?" Red Leader asked through the speaker. "I have orders to launch."

"Absolutely. Positive. I mean affirmative, I guess. I'll explain later. Right now, please do not attack."

"Okay, ma'am. Let's hope you're right. All units, all units, this is Red Leader. Stand down. I repeat, stand down."

Swooping over the *Calypso*, the helicopters banked sharply and left.

CHAPTER 29

The red powerboat pulled up to the docks, again faster than the legally posted speed limit. All three goons hustled up the ramp to the waiting black SUV.

As they were about to drive off, a police car rounded the corner in a power slide, lights flashing and sirens wailing. It screeched to a stop. Police poured out of the car, weapons drawn. Other official vehicles followed close behind.

"Out of the car! All of you! Turn around, hands against the roof! McFarland, search the car."

While handcuffs were applied, Officer McFarland lifted a duffle bag from the backseat of the SUV and unzipped it. Donning gloves, he extracted an automatic rifle. "Whoa! The safety is off!" he exclaimed. "In fact, it's on auto. Someone's going to lose their firearms safety merit badge." He flipped a lever on the side of the rifle, then sniffed the barrel. "It's hot, and it's definitely been fired recently, sir."

"Good work, McFarland. Tag it and bag it as evidence. We've got video of their boat from the choppers."

The officer in charge turned to the three goons. "You're all under arrest for two No Wake Zone violations, a Class Three misdemeanor in this harbor town. You have the right to remain silent…"

Officer McFarland tapped him on the shoulder, whispered in his ear. "Oh right. And for the federal crime of discharging a firearm in the direction of US military aircraft, a felony. We can let you decide who's going to snitch on the actual perpetrator. In the meantime, you're all charged as accomplices. You have the right to remain silent. You have the right to legal counsel. If you cannot afford counsel—and from the looks of this car, you or your boss *can*—it will be provided for you at taxpayer's expense. Et cetera."

The goons were hustled into two police cars and driven away. Other squad cars remained behind, light bars ablaze, pulsing blue lights reflected off the battered, creaking sign hanging in front of the now-boarded-up Spouter Inn. Two officers argued over who would deal with all the paperwork necessary to impound the SUV.

Ashley, Luke, and Clive watched the helicopters disappear over the horizon. Turning back to the monitor, Clive expanded the map as the shark's signal finally disappeared from the screen edge.

"That's as far out as the receiver can pick up the ultrasound signal, so they're at least twenty-plus-miles away and still moving west. We can hope for a surfacing and a radio signal bounce off a satellite, but I'd say they're gone. Mission accomplished, right?"

"Always a dangerous boast, but I agree," Ashley replied.

"What a long, strange trip it's been," Clive said.

"Clive! You like hip-hop, but you're a Deadhead too?"

"Clive, you dog," Luke said, as he peeled up his wetsuit leg and revealed a dancing bear tattoo on his ankle.

"What can I say?" Clive replied, pulling up his trouser leg and displaying his own dancing bear tattoo. "I fell far from the tree."

Ashley smiled again. "Funny, I didn't notice that last night. Well, more importantly, it appears our work here is finished. We should contact the Chinese consulate and tell them we think we found evidence of the missing divers. Then I guess it's time to go home and look for new jobs."

Clive held up his hand. "Yes, but first I have a question. Well, several questions, but let's start with why you thought your harebrained plan would work, that the fins would know to attach to the sharks, that they would find their rightful owners."

"It was admittedly wild speculation. I wasn't worried about the rightful owner thing, because the sharks were clones, meaning they were identical genetically. It shouldn't have been a matter of Fin A finding Shark A, since Sharks A, B, and C were identical. It would be like an organ transplant between identical twins, or triplets, or whatever a dozen clones might be called. That was the easy part. The hard part was whether the fins and the sharks would know to re-connect at all."

"But they did," Luke exclaimed. "It was like automatic, like Magna-Tiles."

"An apt analogy for an adolescent imagination. But you're right. They did connect as if they were pulled together, but it wasn't magnetic. It was more like sponge reassociation."

"I'm lost," Clive said.

"That's probably because your computer background never included a discussion of resurrection in sponges."

"Are we getting into scripture-based biology?" Clive asked.

"No, this is for real, not religious fantasy. It came to me when I remembered the marine biology class I took when I went back to college. The prof waxed poetic about the regenerative properties of sponges, including that, if they've been pushed through a sieve so they're separated into small bits, somehow the bits know to reassemble themselves back into larger chunks of sponge."

"I thought sponges were plastic," Luke said.

"Those are kitchen sponges, Luke. These sponges are animals that live in the ocean."

"Oh."

"Anyway, my thinking was that sponges reproduce by budding off parts to create new sponges, which is another type of parthenogenetic reproduction. Since our sharks had reproduced parthenogenetically, asexually, then maybe, just maybe, they also possessed other attributes of clonal organisms, like regeneration, and maybe even an ability to reassemble. I hoped that the fins would recognize the sharks as something they were a part of."

"That was a stretch," Clive said.

"Absolutely. But what made me hopeful was knowing that sponge reassociation involves collagen-like glue and shark fins are made up of collagen, too."

"I guess the important thing is it worked, far-fetched as it was," Clive admitted.

Luke's attention had wandered as the conversation grew more technical. When it was clear it was over, he rejoined. "Hey, Ashley. You were pretty cool down on the bottom. I'd bet Bubba would be happy to have you as full-time crew on the *Calypso*, if and when we get our license back, and he comes out of hiding."

"Thanks, but no thanks, Luke. I didn't get a PhD in genetics to handhold newbie scuba divers. I guess I could consider going east, where Roper doesn't have contacts. Or start checking want ads."

Clive managed to remove the mooring line from the refuge buoy on the first try, and, with Luke at the wheel, the

Calypso, leaving a trail of its tell-tale black exhaust, headed off in the direction of the speedboat and helicopters. Ashley and Clive stood on the stern, shouting over the engine noise.

"You know, Clive, nothing you do surprises me anymore. I knew you were an electronics whiz and everything, but you really kept your cool when Roper's thugs showed up."

"I don't know. I just tried to stall them while you were playing with the sharks. It was obvious those boys weren't capable of much independent thought or action. They wanted the fins, not us. And you seemed pretty calm."

"Come on. You acted like it was no big thing, those dimwits waving that gun around. I would have been totally freaked, but your calmness really helped me keep most of my cool."

"Maybe I should have been more scared," Clive said.

"No, it was brains *and* bravery. I think you were just plain awesome." She gave him another kiss, longer than the last.

The *Calypso* pulled up to the dock to find police cars with lights flashing and the KNSX reporting team set up, complete with satellite uplink truck.

"Oops," Clive said. "I guess my parole officer is more efficient than I thought. Kind of seems like overkill, don't you think?"

Several police officers ran down the ramp and helped tie the boat up. The three crusaders got off the boat and were greeted by intrepid reporter Stan Daily, microphone in hand, backed by a camerawoman.

"Here come the heroes of the moment right now," Daily announced, looking at the camera. He shoved the microphone in a clearly puzzled Ashley's face.

"I'm here with Dr. Ashley Worth of AlphaGen Technologies. Dr. Worth, how did you get the sharks to leave?"

"Huh? What? How did you know that? What's this all about?"

"The captain of the helicopter squadron reported to the mayor about your radio call that made them abort their mission to bomb the sharks. They reported a school of giant killer sharks swimming west, away from the shore. The mayor called KNSX News. You've saved our city."

"Actually, we were mostly trying to save the sharks."

Inside the uplink truck, a news producer in front of a control console talked to Daily via his earbud. "Stan, we're on tape delay and can splice that out. Let's take it from 'The mayor called KNSX News,' and you say, 'You've saved the day.'"

After a brief pause, during which it was obvious he was listening to something, Daily parroted, "You've saved the day."

Ashley, catching on, went along. "Oh, it was really a team effort. We had figured out that all the sharks really wanted was to get their fins back, which was what we did."

"And exactly how did you figure that out? It couldn't have been easy."

"Well, the process was fairly straightforward. I ran a standard analysis for the 648 base-pair region in the mitochondrial cytochrome c oxidase 1 gene to see if the sharks were somehow related. We found that all of these particular sharks were sisters and had been produced parthenogenetically."

The producer spoke again into Daly's earbud. "We'll cut and splice that to 'I ran a standard analysis to find out if the sharks were related.'"

"And were they?" Daily asked, winking at Ashley.

"Absolutely. They were identical clones. This led me, er, us, to think they were exceptional. The link was their missing fins. Clearly, everyone could see from your TV footage of the attacks that these sharks had missing fins. They attacked the kind of people and boats that had cut their fins off. Your news broadcasts were the key."

The uplink producer told Daily, "Let's push that one. The advertisers will eat it up."

"Serving the public, that's always our goal," Daily said, after a moment's hesitation. "And how is it that you were able to get their missing fins? That couldn't have been as straightforward."

Ashley stopped a moment, trying to decide how much to reveal. Finally, she said, "I'm afraid that's a matter we'll have to take up with the local authorities. I wouldn't want to compromise a possible criminal investigation."

"Oh, of course." Daily turned back and faced the camera. "Clearly there's more to this story than we know right now, so stay tuned. This is KNSX reporter Stan Daily, signing off for now. Back to you, Earl."

As soon as Daily left, a police officer and a tall man in a dark suit walked up to the three.

"Dr. Worth, I'm Agent Longfellow with US Customs and Border Protection. We're starting to put some pieces together here and are very interested in getting a statement from you. Would you mind coming downtown with us?"

"Sure," Ashley responded. "As long as all three of us get to go, after we change into dry clothes."

"I don't think that's a problem. We can wait."

Luke hung back. "Is it okay if I take *Calypso* to her berth and clean things up from our dive? I promised Bubba I'd take care of her while he's away."

Ashley knew Luke was never really comfortable around law enforcement, given his recreational pastimes. "Sure, Luke. If they need a statement from you, I'll let you know."

CHAPTER 30

Police vehicles, lightbars ablaze and sirens wailing, pulled up to the AlphaGen building. Following protocol, some officers entered the building, while others placed crime scene tape around the outside. Boxes were carried out of the building, one policewoman carrying Roper's computer. The evidence was placed in a police van, which drove off, along with a few police vehicles. Two policemen and one vehicle stayed behind. Lab techs in white lab coats milled around outside the building, watching the action.

Later that day, a convoy of police vehicles, rooftop lightbars flashing, pulled up to the warehouse where Ashley and her accomplices escaped from the dogs. What looked like a SWAT team, armed to the teeth, rushed into the building, weapons drawn. Other officers encircled the warehouse with crime scene tape.

Shortly after, several police exited the building carrying boxes, eyes watering and heads turned to avoid the odor. The evidence was placed in a police van. This included the sawfish snout, held tentatively by a policewoman, who was trying not to impale herself on the protruding saw teeth.

With flashing lights and sirens, the van drove off, followed by more police vehicles. Two policemen and one vehicle remained behind.

Rowdy Wagner had been on his way to the warehouse in his black Jeep. Agatha had asked him to check up on some scuttlebutt she'd heard around the docks about hanky-panky concerning shark fins. Arriving a little later than the armada and seeing all the police activity ahead, he pulled into an alley a few buildings up the street. Crouching down out of sight behind the Jeep, he saw the boxes being loaded into the van. He took out his phone and made a call, waited for the police vehicles to leave, and drove off.

CHAPTER 31

At the international concourse of the regional airport, a gate attendant with a distinctive Caribbean accent announced, "For those passengers waiting for Caicos Air Flight 14 to the Turks and Caicos, we apologize for the delay. We had some minor issues with the plane's interior following the inbound flight that we've now corrected. We certainly want you to have the most comfortable conditions possible on your flight to Providenciales, so we hope you will forgive the wait. We're now ready to board our first class and business class passengers. We'll begin general boarding in a few minutes."

Passengers began lining up at the gate podium. Among them was D. W. Roper in an expensive suit. Farther back stood a tall man in a dark suit, white shirt, and dark tie: Agent Longfellow. Three other men in dark suits, with curly wires dangling from their earpieces, followed Longfellow. They were the last first-class passengers allowed to board.

Roper took a window seat in first class and settled in. A minute later, Agent Longfellow sat down in the aisle seat next to him, took several colorful travel brochures from his carry-on, and placed them in the seat pocket ahead of him. He turned to Roper.

"Excuse me. I forgot to check. Do they take US dollars in the Turks and Caicos?"

"Yeah."

Roper reached into a travel bag and took out a pair of headphones and began to put them on. Longfellow interrupted.

"Great. Thanks. Stupid of me not to check ahead of time. You've reassured me. By the way, my name's Longfellow, Robert Longfellow."

Longfellow reached over to shake hands. Roper gave it a cursory shake.

"Russel. David Russel," Roper mumbled.

He placed the headphones on and turned toward the window.

"Pleasure to meet you, Mr. Russel," Longfellow said to himself. He nodded to a flight attendant standing by the entry door, who had been observing carefully.

Lifting the announcement phone from its cradle, he said, "If a Mr. David Russel is on board, will he please push the flight attendant call button over his seat." When Roper didn't respond, he nodded at Longfellow and repeated, "Mr. David Russel?"

Longfellow tapped Roper lightly on the shoulder, indicating for him to take his headphones off.

"Excuse me, but I think they're trying to get your attention."

Roper looked surprised, annoyed. He reached up and pushed the call button. The flight attendant walked over, smiling.

"Mr. Russel? Oh good. I'm sorry, but there seems to be some mix-up with a tag on your checked luggage. I don't have any details. Would you mind terribly stepping to the front of the plane for a moment while we let other passengers get on board?"

Roper, clearly put out, stood.

Longfellow got up and let Roper into the aisle, then followed him to the front of the plane. The dark-suited men with the curly wire earpieces were next to board. When Roper saw them, he turned around quickly and bumped into Longfellow.

"Dexter W. Roper, you are under arrest. You are charged with violating Food and Drug Administration regulations concerning falsification of food origin labeling, as a codefendant in laws regarding illegal shark finning, as the instigator of the attack on Ms. Florence Takata, and for traveling with a false passport. You have the right to…"

While Longfellow was reading Roper his rights, one of the agents roughly pulled his arms behind his back and placed the cuffs on. Longfellow spun him around and all five left the plane, Longfellow thanking the flight attendant for his cooperation.

At the same airport and concourse a few hours later, on board a plane bound for Hong Kong, Longfellow and three dark-suited men with the curly wire earpieces confront a well-dressed Asian passenger.

"Robert Chang," Longfellow announced. "You are under arrest. You are charged with violating federal and state laws involving illegal possession of shark fins, the Federal Lacey and Endangered Species Acts concerning trafficking in endangered species, and for attempting to travel with a false passport. You have the right to…"

While Longfellow was reading him his rights, one of the agents deftly pulled Chang's arms behind his back and placed cuffs on. Longfellow turned him around and all five left the plane, Longfellow thanking a flight attendant for her cooperation.

CHAPTER 32

Agatha was behind the wheelhouse of the *Wrinkle*, holding a hose and directing a powerful stream of water at the stern deck below. Three police vehicles pulled up to the dock, lights flashing. Uniformed men and women hurried down a gangplank to where the boat was tied up. One officer, holding a sheaf of papers, shouted up to Agatha, who took her time turning off the water.

"Agatha Garmin?"

"Yes, officer. What can I do for you?"

"Ms. Garmin, I have a warrant to search your vessel. I don't need permission to come aboard."

"You have it anyway. I always do my best to cooperate with the authorities. Just be careful. Fishing boats tend to be slippery. Can I get anyone some coffee?"

Several policemen and one policewoman climbed on the boat and dispersed. Some lifted hatch covers and peered inside, others looked under tarps and inside fish boxes. All were empty and spotless. The officer in charge and another climbed up the ladder to the wheelhouse and rummaged around while Agatha leaned on her walking stick and lit her pipe.

"Here, Sarge. Is this what you were looking for?" The accompanying officer picked up a leather-bound book and handed it to the officer in charge. On the cover was written, "Logbook, *Stinky Wrinkle*."

"Ms. Garman, is this your official catch record?"

"Yes, sir. I think it's pretty up-to-date. Would you like some explanation for the entries? Some of it's kinda shorthand."

"That won't be necessary. We are taking it as evidence."

He pulled a small, black, official-looking notebook from his back pocket, wrote quickly, and tore off a page that he handed to Agatha. "This is a receipt for your catch record book. It'll be downtown at headquarters."

"Thanks. I hope you can get that back to me pronto. We're fishing tonight, and I'm out of compliance if I don't have that on board and current."

"We'll do our best. I advise you to not go too far. We may need to contact you further."

Agatha accompanied the two officers down the ladder to where the other police were lounging around on the deck, checking out the fishing gear.

"Hey, Sarge," one said. "We've looked pretty much everywhere. Haven't found a damn thing. This boat is empty."

"Well, you know, boys," Agatha said, a smile on her face, "I have a reputation for keeping a clean ship. You shouldn't be surprised."

Sarge grunted, looked at Agatha skeptically. "Okay. Let's go," he said, disappointment clear in his voice. "We'll probably be back."

One of the officers was holding a roll of partially unspooled yellow crime scene tape.

"For chrissake, put that away!"

As they were about to leave, the lone policewoman in the raiding crew tried to catch the officer in charge's attention.

"Sarge?"

"What is it, Lopez?"

She walked over and whispered into Sarge's ear. He

looked at her with mild contempt, then finally said, "Sure. What the hell."

"Captain Garmin," she said to Agatha. "Can I get a photo of you standing near that big drum? This is my first search, and I want to scrapbook it for my daughter."

Agatha was only too happy to oblige, hamming it up a little.

"Hey, isn't that the club you used to whack those sharks during the boat parade? You're pretty lethal with that thing."

Agatha posed proudly, taking a batter's stance, as if her knobby club were a baseball bat. Lopez snapped away until Sarge got impatient.

"Alright already. Can we leave now?" he asked.

"Yes, sir. Thank you, ma'am."

"Ta. Anytime. Careful getting off my boat now."

Lopez was riding shotgun in Sarge's car.

"What the hell was that all about?" he demanded. "This has to be at least your twentieth search, and I know for a fact you don't have a daughter."

"Right," Lopez answered. "Nor do I scrapbook. But before I decided to go to the police academy, I got a degree in biology. One of the classes I took was mammalogy, the study of mammals. In lab, we had to learn to identify different animals by their bones. You know, skull, teeth, random leg and arm bones, stuff like that. The prof was particularly proud of his collection of bacula."

"Say what?" Sarge asked, indignantly.

"Bacula. That's plural for baculum. More coarsely, os penis."

"Whose penis?"

"Os penis is the penile bone. Many mammals are gifted with one, like dogs (medium size), raccoons (toothpick size), bears (big), walruses (even bigger). Chimps and gorillas have one, although we humans don't, unfortunately. Nor do elephants nor whales. Too heavy, I guess."

"And?" Sarge muttered impatiently.

"And," Lopez continued. "Our prof bragged extensively about his baculum collection, like, he used raccoon bacula as swizzle sticks. He said Alaskan indigenes have a special name for one, call it an *oosik*. They polish fossilized walrus bacula and turn them into handles for knives and other tools. There's even a poem called 'Ode to an Oosik' that starts something like 'Strange things have been done in the Midnight Sun…'"

"Stop! Where is this going, Lopez?"

"I'll spell it out, Sarge. Agatha's little walking stick is a walrus baculum, an oosik, no doubt about it. Which is a violation of the Marine Mammal Protection Act, which we also learned can result in a fine of $100,000 and a year's imprisonment. That was a question on the final. I now have photographic proof of her possession of one. We didn't find any shark fins, which would violate the Shark Fin Sales Elimination Act of 2021 and would have been great, but at least we can get her for possessing an oosik!"

Sarge performed a power slide, 180-degree skidding turn and accelerated, forcing a following patrol car off the road.

"Hold on, Sarge. What are you doing?"

"We're going back to arrest her for possession of a… dracula or abacus or whatever."

"We can't, Sarge. Our warrant specifically stated we were searching for shark fins. We'll have to go back to the judge and get a new one for the baculum." She said the final word very slowly.

"Damn, you're right."

"I've got to email my old mammalogy prof. He's going to be so stoked."

Epilogue

"I'm just not a fan of sharks."
DONALD J. TRUMP

A run-down fishing boat, white with numerous rust stains, idled noisily on the glassy water. Sunlight filtered by diesel exhaust revealed *Stinky Wrinkle* in fading black letters across its stern. To the left of the name in new black paint, the letters "R/V" had been hastily added. No home port.

Luke and Rowdy stood on the stern of the *Wrinkle*, staring down at the water, where an international orange float bobbed in the gentle swell, revealing its attachment to the end of a fishing longline. Both men wore yellow bib overalls and white rubber boots. Rowdy dragged on a cigarette.

The float disappeared under the water and zigzagged erratically.

"FISH ON!" Rowdy shouted.

Leaping into action, Rowdy winched in the fishing line, bringing up a large shark. Hands and arms belonging to Ashley and Clive reached over the side and gently slid the shark into a sling behind the boat. Rowdy rolled the thrashing shark onto its back, at which point it stopped struggling.

"Okay," Ashley said. "It's gone into tonic immobility, just like the literature says it should. Tag time."

Clive stuck a running seawater hose into the mouth of the upside-down shark. Rowdy measured the shark. Ashley recorded data.

Clive clipped an electronic tag onto the dorsal fin. As Ashley pulled out the hose, Rowdy cut the hook with bolt cutters. They rolled the shark onto its belly and tipped the animal into the water. The shark righted itself and swam off, slowly at first, then disappeared with a flick of its tail.

Agatha was standing at the back of the wheelhouse, overseeing the action, stopwatch in hand. "Good work, crew. Forty-five seconds, our fastest tag yet. Not bad for a virgin research vessel. The *Wrinkle* is earning her new initials. And I'm sure happy to have you on board, Luke."

"Hey, this beats kissing butts for tips, and I like working on a boat that will actually get me home."

The crew baited and tossed the fishing gear back overboard.

"I bet my school buddies at Caltech would be blown away if they knew I was a shark fisherman, not to mention my home boys back in the 'hood,'" Clive said to Ashley, as they stood together near the stern of the Wrinkle.

"Seamless code-switch there, Clive," Ashley quipped.

"Sometimes the vernacular just slips out, exposing my roots," Clive said.

"You seem more than comfortable in either world. But I'm glad you're in this one. Mostly," she added.

"Thanks. Me too," Clive said.

"Anyway," Ashley continued. "Things have really turned around since we saved the sharks."

"Don't you mean the city," he corrected.

"Oh, right, of course. Gotta maintain the narrative. So much has happened since those goons pinned all the blame on Roper. I guess they were motivated to cooperate when they found out what kind of jail time they were facing. They were only too happy to toss Roper under the bus."

"They had the right to remain silent," Clive said. "But it looks like they exercised their First Amendment rights instead."

"They weren't alone. Almost as quickly, Roper ratted out Chang."

"No honor amongst thieves, I guess," Clive said.

"Certainly not those thieves," Ashley remarked.

Luke tired of staring at the float and breathing Rowdy's cigarette smoke. He walked over to Ashley and Clive. "Hey guys," he said. "I missed a lot of the fun 'cause I had to refill the dive tanks, wash down the gear, and fuel the boat, before I went home. Can you fill me in on what happened when we landed minus our sharky buddies?"

Ashley smiled and said, "Right. We went back to the boat because the customs officials wanted to talk to you, but we couldn't find you. I guess you'd left. But it didn't matter. Turns out your testimony wasn't needed after all. The wheels of justice started turning real fast when Roper got busted trying to flee the country. He willingly provided details about Chang's warehouse, where they found a bunch more fins, plus rhino horn, tiger testicles, and your sawfish snout. It looks like Happy Charlie Seafood has been a major smuggler of endangered species. It's one of the biggest illegal animal trade busts ever. And we're getting a lot of the credit," she said with considerable pride.

"We have met the enemy, and it's the profit motive," Clive said. "I heard that those goons copped a plea when the police found chunks of Flo's paint on one of their cars. They reduced their jail time by squealing on Roper for hiring them as hit men. Flo's data nailed Roper's coffin shut on the Golden Tilapia scam. It's against FDA regulations to fake where food comes from. So now Chinese tilapia will stay Chinese, thanks especially to Flo. Clearly, hell hath no fury as a timid technician scorned."

"Yes, hooray for Flo. But don't forget Talulah," Ashley interjected. "We wouldn't have known all the twists and turns if it hadn't been for her. She sort of made a habit of listening in on phone calls between Roper and Chang and turned out to be a star witness for the prosecution."

"Yes, the sistah got included, whether or not Roper intended it," Clive said.

Ashley nodded in agreement. "Talulah takes her responsibility as the collective conscience of AlphaGen seriously. She provided evidence that Roper and Chang had been joined at the hip for a long time. Roper owed Chang a chunk of money, because Chang loaned him the funds to start AlphaGen. Roper's credit score was in the single digits. No one would lend him cash, given his lack of genetic tech background, plus some previous shady dealings. When Roper couldn't pay Chang back, Chang extorted him into fronting the shark fin trade, as well as running the Golden Tilapia scam."

"My guess," Clive offered, "is that Roper didn't need a lot of convincing, once he saw the profit margins and immediate payback."

"Probably so," Ashley responded. "Golden Tilapia was supposed to be Roper's cash cow, get him out of debt. But the necessary research, what I was doing, took time, and neither Roper nor Chang are patient people. So now Roper is maintaining his innocence on the basis of being blackmailed. Pretty contorted argument, but he wants a jury trial.

As befits someone with his ego, he's not hiring a lawyer. He's going to convince the jury on his own."

"What's the old legal adage?" Clive chuckled. "A man who defends himself in court has a fool for a client."

Ashley's phone chirped. She pulled it out, looked at the number, puzzled. "Uh, hello… Yes, it is… As good a time as any."

She listened, nodded, said yes several times, then shut her phone, smiling.

"What was that all about?" Clive asked.

"Someone wanting to know if I was interested in an extended warranty for my VW."

"Huh?" Luke asked.

"Just kidding," Ashley said. "All this publicity must be a good thing. That was AlphaGen's competitor, TechnoGen. They're offering me a job improving crop yields in developing countries."

"A deft move through the transfer portal, to a better team," Clive quipped.

"Basically," Ashley replied. "And because of my journalism background, they're upping my salary. Most scientists can't write a believable absence excuse note for their kids."

"Hey, congrats, Ashley, that's great. Everybody's taken care of, even Admiral Garmin up there, sort of," Clive said as he looked up at Agatha, who was smoking a pipe. Noticeably missing was her walking stick. "She almost got off scot-free because they never found her with any fins. It looks like someone tipped her off about a raid." Clive looked at Rowdy. "I wonder who that could have been."

Rowdy suddenly realized the fishing gear needed tending.

Clive looked back at Ashley. "Agatha dodged and weaved through a number of legal challenges and, unlike

Roper, hired a good lawyer. Officialdom thought they could convict her because of her walking stick, which was from a walrus pen...er, body part," Clive mumbled the last part. "Walruses are protected by federal law. But she claimed she got it in Alaska when the *Wrinkle* was up north fishing for salmon. Bought it from an Alaskan native, and they're exempted from that protection. She couldn't produce a receipt, so all that happened was the stick was confiscated and given to a museum."

"She's slipperier than goose shit," Luke said.

"Almost," Clive replied. "She finally lost her commercial license because her confiscated logbook didn't mention sharks, but it did list flounder when flounder were out of season. She also got cited for crashing into the dock during the boat parade. They busted her for reckless boat operation and damaging public property. The *Wrinkle* got impounded and given to a shark research nonprofit when she couldn't pay the hefty reparations. Her lawyer brokered a deal with the nonprofit, citing her exceptional prowess at shark fishing. In lieu of jail time, she's catching sharks for science. And here we are, happily aiding and abetting."

"I guess that's some kind of justice, given the sharks were the cause of everything in the first place," Ashley commented.

"At least she's being watched now. But here's actual good news. I learned this morning that my copyright infringement conviction has been overturned and my record cleared because of my role in nailing Roper."

"So now what?" Ashley asked. "Your skills must be wanted by someone."

"Right. I'm still a hot commodity. The folks who did the *Westworld* animatronics have asked me to build a young

Justin Bieber doll. And they have lawyers to protect me."

Ashley smiled at Clive. "Depending on how anatomically correct that doll is, I may rethink having you as a roommate."

Luke was still fixated on the sawfish snout and other stuff taken in the warehouse raid. "So, what do people use tiger balls for, anyway?" he asked.

"I think it's supposed to enhance their virility," Ashley answered.

"Their what?"

"Their sexual performance."

"Isn't Viagra more effective?" Clive asked.

"Maybe their doctors won't give them a prescription," Luke suggested.

"Fat chance," Ashley said.

Afterword

D. W. Roper was arraigned on state and federal charges related to FDA regulations, shark fin sales, attempted murder, and passport falsification. He pled not guilty on all counts and requested the charges be dropped. Losing that argument, he asked for a change of venue, which the judge also denied. The only argument he won was for setting bond, based on his lack of a criminal record. The judge granted bond, but initially set bail at one million dollars, citing his effort to flee to the Turks and Caicos, thus making him a flight risk. He maintained he was only going there to liquidate funds for future, beneficial genetic experimentation. The judge had difficulty hiding her amusement, upped the bond to 1.5 million, and required him to wear an ankle tracking bracelet.

Roper posted bail after selling his holdings in AlphaGen to rival TechnoGen, the company that hired Ashley. He paid one last, late-night visit to the AlphaGen labs, to clear out his office. His remaining possessions included the partially consumed bottle of Chivas Regal.

Loading things into his authentic, three million dollar 1968 Ford Mustang GT—the muscle car featured in the Steve McQueen movie *Bullitt*—he sped out of the AlphaGen parking lot and toward home. He took a long pull on the Chivas bottle, accelerated, and approached the sharp left curve that was clearly marked by a black-on-yellow curved traffic arrow attached to a large oak tree.

Attempting to downshift to reduce speed, his ankle bracelet caught on the brake pedal. The car, now in neutral, careened forward. He slammed on the brakes and twisted the steering wheel hard left, to no avail. The Mustang skidded and crashed sideways into the oak tree, acorns raining down on the crumpled car like golden-brown hailstones. Being authentic, the car lacked air bags.

The squirrel—jolted awake by the impact—couldn't believe his good luck.

THE END

Acknowledgments

FINS was originally conceived as a screenplay called *Undead Sharks*. I wrote it to fulfill a desire to right a wrong, namely to counter the influence of the hyped, sensationalist, grossly unfair portrayal of sharks in a few novels, notably *Jaws* and later, *The Meg*. Additional damage has been done via many sharksploitation movies, beginning with *Jaws*, which fathered an onslaught of wannabes, including, but not limited to, *The Meg* and, of course, *Sharknado,* in all its incarnations. As with the vast majority of screenplays, *Undead Sharks* languished, unproduced, despite some pretty good results in screenplay contests. Maybe the world wasn't quite ready for a shark-friendly rendition of an old favorite.

FINS emerged because the story was already there, albeit in shortened form due to the 110-page restriction placed on screenplays. Clearly, it needed to be fleshed out. Writing *FINS* was also a way to escape the distasteful task of promoting my well-received, award-winning orca novel, *Beyond the Human Realm*. Writing is fun, marketing is mind-numbing.

I knew from the start that *FINS* would appeal to a very different audience than the orca novel. Although still ecofiction, *FINS* lacks the emotional weight. From the beginning, *FINS* was meant to be frivolous, a parody on the sharksploitation genre, borrowing heavily from scenes, elements, and ideas reworked to death in that genre. Fans of shark horror stories will recognize the conceit, fans of *Beyond the Human Realm* will wonder what happened, where I went astray. Barnacle glue and a yellow VW beetle are the only vestiges of that earlier effort. I apologize to anyone expecting a sequel to the orca book. That remains a work in progress.

Undead Sharks, and later *FINS*, was fiction, based on a certain amount of science, facts acquired during my lifelong fascination with sharks and detailed in my coauthored shark reference book, *Sharks: The Animal Answer Guide*. Many of the moments in *FINS* are poorly disguised rip-offs of sharksploitation books and movies. I remain unapologetic.

Both shark stories profited greatly from the editorial comments and abundant criticisms of many patient readers, including Rick Brusca, (who introduced me to the idea of sponge reassociation as a possible means—albeit still unlikely—of reuniting the sharks with their fins), Nancy Wolf (grammarian extraordinaire), Howard Schein (innumerable, essential changes), Frank May (great at spotting redundancies and providing alternative scenarios), Brian Bowen (who tried to keep me honest with genetic terminology and practices), Shannon Cave (who undercharges for what she advertises as copyediting, shannoncaveediting@gmail.com), Vita Rose (responsible for the cover image!), Mike Flanagan, Geael Peter Lawrence, Judy Meyer (who keeps me almost honest in general), Devon Helfmeyer (legal jargon interpreter), Russell Engelman (thorough, knowledgeable, helpful), Harold Van Doren, George Benz, Shawn Miller, Luanna Helfman, Patricia and Dany Hubalek, Dovi Kacev, David Shiffman, JoeAnn Hart, Ric Martini, Ralph

Collier, Katherine Maslenikov, Ron Carrol, Greg Skomal, M. A. Marks, Jeff Carrier, George Burgess, Greg Cailliet, Larry Allen, Larry Dill, and several anonymous contest judges (who could have changed the world). I admittedly high-graded and cherry-picked their suggested corrections, comments, and criticisms. I thank them for their efforts. I own all the errors in the book. They tried.

The good people at Luminare Press were once again a pleasure to work with, smoothing the waters of the publishing process. They were particularly helpful at masterfully transforming my sister's idea for the cover art into something I love to look at, and at shepherding my effort through from beginning to end with admirable professionalism.

And, if you happen to know someone in the movie business looking for a revolutionary take on the shark horror genre, I'm ready to update that effort on short notice. Contact me at genehelfman@gmail.com, even if you just want to chat about the book, life, or shark (or orca) conservation. Also, visit my probably-out-of-date website, https://gene-helfman.pubsitepro.com/.

And *please*, don't hesitate to review *FINS* on Amazon and/or Goodreads and recommend it to your local library. We need to get the word out.

About the Author

GENE HELFMAN, PHD, is an animal behaviorist turned conservation biologist. He has authored four reference books on fish and marine conservation. His 2021 novel, Beyond the Human Realm—about love, loss, and redemption among killer whales—won the 2022 NIEA Award and 2022 Readers' Favorite Award for Animal Fiction. Gene and his wife Dr. Judy Meyer live on Lopez Island in Washington State.

For more information, visit:
GENEHELFMAN.PUBSITEPRO.COM

Made in United States
Orlando, FL
03 October 2023